SIMONE WEIL

SIMONE WEIL

Attention to

THE REAL

ROBERT CHENAVIER

Translated by

BERNARD E. DOERING

University of Notre Dame Press

Notre Dame, Indiana

Manufactured in the United States of America

Original title: *Simone Weil, l'attention au réel*
1ère édition en France en 2009 aux Éditions Michalon
Copyright © Robert Chenavier, 2009
Tous droits réservés

Library of Congress Cataloging-in-Publication Data

Chenavier, Robert.
[Simone Weil, l'attention au réel. English]
Simone Weil, attention to the real / Robert Chenavier ; translated by
Bernard E. Doering.
p.   cm.
Includes bibliographical references (p.   ).
ISBN-13: 978-0-268-02373-7 (pbk. : alk. paper)
ISBN-10: 0-268-02373-5 (pbk. : alk. paper)
ISBN-13: 978-0-268-07688-7 (ebook)
1. Weil, Simone, 1909-1943. I. Title.
B2430.W474C4813   2012
194—dc23
2012025739

To my wife Jane, *dimidium animae,*

Without whose generous help and long-suffering patience
This translation would never have been realized.

contents

Simone Weil's *L'Enracinement* caught my attention in the 1950s shortly after its first publication. This provocative author had developed her plan for the political and social reform of France after World War II during her wartime exile with the Free France in London. Over the succeeding years, the principal subject of my research has been the French philosopher Jacques Maritain, but my interest in Weil continued.

Years later, my wife Jane chose the political thought of Simone Weil for a presentation during her doctoral studies at Northwestern University. Deeply impressed by what she learned about this young philosopher, she wrote her dissertation on Weil's political, social, and historical writings. At the Bibliothèque nationale in Paris, with the generous help and encouragement of Florence de Lussy, curator of the Fonds Simone Weil, she found a mother lode of published and unpublished material by the young philosopher: personal reflections, essays, articles in prominent or obscure periodicals, plans for articles, class notes, general notes, correspondence with her students and with literary and political personages, even a play. In the process of becoming a Weil scholar, she assiduously mined the works of Simone Weil and has produced two books and numerous articles for the *Cahiers Simone Weil* as well as annual conference presentations at both the American Simone Weil Society and the European Association pour l'Etude de la Pensée de Simone Weil.

Over the years, while accompanying my wife on her annual pilgrimages to the meetings of these two societies in America and in Europe, my knowledge of this fascinating philosopher gradually increased, though in a rather spasmodic and disorganized fashion. As I listened to numerous presentations, my admiration for Weil deepened. At the 2009 meeting in Angers, France, I purchased a small book, *L'Attention au Réel* (Paris: Editions Michalon), published that same year by Robert Chenavier, president of the French Simone Weil Association, which I read on the flight home.

This concise account of the life of Simone Weil, with its clear, sympathetic, and organized introduction to her thought and its development, was just what I needed. Because of what this little book did for me, I decided to translate it into English for the benefit of those who want to know more about this fascinating philosopher. In the text I have provided the original French sources given by Robert Chenavier, and I have added English sources of these same citations whenever they were readily available, which was far from simple given that translators selected and put together texts from various collections and from different periods of Weil's life. Some of the sources have not yet been translated, and many of those translated do not include the entire original text. All translations of the citations in *Attention to the Real* are my own and thus often differ in wording from the existing translations. The sources of the available English versions accompany the sources of the French citations in the text and are identified according to the list of abbreviations given on the following page.

Bernard E. Doering

abbreviations

Works in English inserted in the text

FW   *Formative Writings, 1929–1941*

IC   *Intimations of Christianity among the Ancient Greeks* (chapters from *Intuitions pré-chrétiennes* and *La Source Grecque*)

LP   *Letter to a Priest*

NR   *The Need for Roots*

OL   *Oppression and Liberty*

SE   *Selected Essays*

SL   *Seventy Letters*

SNL   *On Science, Necessity, and the Love of God*

SWA   *Simone Weil, An Anthology*

SWL   *Simone Weil, A Life*

SWR   *The Simone Weil Reader*

SWS   *Simone Weil,* Selected Writings

WG   *Waiting for God*

Bury yourself in an obscure life:

Whatever sprouts before being placed in the earth

Never comes to maturity.

Hikam, *Paroles de sagesse.*

Act in such a way that you may be a source of mercy

for others, even if God has made of you a trial for yourself.

Junayd, *Enseignement spirituel.*

Introduction

To Marie Noël

At the time of her death in 1943 at the age of thirty-four, Simone Weil had already shown in the conduct of her life a responsibility at once intellectual, moral, and political, which brought to her writings an interior need for coherence, even if her work did not take on the form of a system.

From a philosophical point of view, it is difficult to classify her doctrine. On the one hand she affirms that, in her eyes, "nothing surpasses Plato" (*Pensees sans ordre,* 66; SL, 131). On the other hand the place reserved for Plato and Greece in the interpretation of her thought must not overshadow what she wrote in 1934 in *Réflexions sur les causes de la liberté et l'oppression sociale*: "The notion of work considered as a human value is without a doubt the single spiritual conquest that human thought has made since the Greek miracle; this was perhaps the only lacuna in the ideal of human thought that Greece elaborated" (*Oeuvres complètes* II.2.92;

OL, 106). She would return to this subject in 1943, insisting that "our epoch has for its mission the establishment of a civilization founded on the spirituality of work," the thoughts related to the "premonition of this vocation" being the only ones "that we did not borrow from the Greeks" (*L'Enracinement*, 125; NR, 96).

These two citations should be enough to explain another constant presence in the thought of Simone Weil, that of Marx, a presence justified in a critical way by a serious lack: "A philosophy [of work] has still to be elaborated," and in this direction Marx "did not begin even the outline of a rough sketch" (*Oppression et liberté*, 223; OL, 169). "Plato expressed only the half of it" (*Oeuvres complètes* VI.1.424) and Marx left only a "few indications" (*Oppression et liberté*, 223; OL, 169) for elaborating an authentic materialism. Platonism cannot be complete without according its proper place to a philosophy of work, and no materialism can be coherent without admitting the reality of the supernatural. Weil took great pains to reduce the opposition between a Plato whose theory of knowledge would have integrated the domain of work and a Marx who would have developed the most precious elements of his materialism by preserving the reality of the supernatural. Having arrived at this crossroad of thought, she carefully avoided neglecting either of the two paths.

This is how Weil defined the "interior necessity" which guided her: "For me personally life had no other meaning, and fundamentally has never had any other meaning, than waiting for truth" (*Ecrits de Londres*, 213; SL, 178). As a disciple of Plato, which she never ceased to be, she told her pupils that truth "is the light of the sun . . . ; it comes from the Good, which illuminates its value" (*Oeuvres complètes* I, 398). One could imagine this philosopher addressing her beginning students as the only ones in a position to leave the cave and choose a life of pure conceptual speculation. It was not this way at all. How did Weil succeed in reconciling an intellectual and spiritual vocation, the object of which was to lift the veil from truth, with an existence exposed to the realities of this world during the very period when spiritual preoccupations dominated her thought?

A formula from her notebooks answers this question: truth "is always experimental" (*Oeuvres complètes* VI.4.177). There is neither empiricism nor pragmatism in such a statement; experience is defined as the "exploration" of different levels of reality. To these levels of being correspond degrees of knowledge, of "reading," says Simone Weil. One might also say of "attention," a key notion defined from the time of her first writings as a way of being active, a grasp of things found by thought (*Oeuvres complètes* I, 275). Truth is the work of "pure thought" (398), but this purity requires an operation of purification, before establishing contact with . . . With what exactly? It is not certain that this truth can be *spoken,* that it arises from the discursive intelligence. To affirm that truth is the object of love or of passion is not a fitting expression, for it is "always the truth of some thing": "What one loves is something that exists, that one thinks, and for this reason could be the occasion of truth or of error" (*L'Enracinement,* 319; NR, 253). Nor does she hesitate to write that "truth is the radiance of reality." It is a principle of order, comparable to light, which is not visible but which makes visible: it is the "nameless point (*alogos*) according to which one can establish order" (*Oeuvres complètes* VI.2.210), organize objects on several levels, without itself being an object. Philosophy, according to Simone Weil, is that practical task of *reading* on different levels, thanks to an orientation of one's gaze toward the truth, established as the principle that puts in place the different contacts that we have with the real.

chapter one

Concerning the "Real Life"
in the "Land of the Real"

To an exceptional degree, the life of Simone Weil, her personality, her commitment, and her reflection form one single whole. She was born in Paris on February 3, 1909, three years after her brother André, a noted mathematician, who died in 1998. Her father, a doctor, was descended from a Jewish family long established in Alsace. Her maternal grandmother was very attached to Judaism, but Simone's father was an atheist. Simone's mother was born in Rostov-on-the-Don. Her family left Russia in 1882, at the time of the first pogroms. This was a family of "liberal Jews" little known for their religious practice, who showed a pronounced taste for the fine arts. If her brother's exceptional gifts were a source of emulation for the brilliant student that Simone was, they seemed also to have had distressing consequences for her psychological evolution. *Attente de Dieu* contains a letter to Father Perrin about this painful experience: feeling that she would prefer to die rather than live without the truth.

At the age of sixteen, she entered the preparatory class for the *grandes écoles* at the celebrated secondary school Lycée Henri IV. Alain, her professor of philosophy, nicknamed her "la Martienne." She wore thick glasses and a questioning look and dressed in clothes of a masculine cut. Her classmates called her intransigent, rude, and even unbearable. Her declared pacifist convictions, the classes she taught to railroad workers in a "social education group," and her militancy led the director of the Ecole normale supérieur to name her "the red virgin." When she received the coveted rank of *agrégation* in philosophy in 1931, she had already told her friend Simone Pétrement of her plan to seek work in a factory.

While she was teaching in the secondary school at Le Puy for the school year 1931–32, she lived very modestly, keeping from her salary only the equivalent of what an elementary school teacher earned. The rest she distributed to the funds for the unemployed and to the treasury of the mineworkers' union in Saint-Etienne. She ate very little and did not heat her apartment because, as she said, those without jobs do not have the money to buy coal. She already suffered from violent and long-lasting migraines. As a full-time teacher at the Le Puy lycée, this young professor also prepared classes for the miners at their trade union meetings in Saint-Etienne, was active in union militancy, and collaborated on several small periodicals—following up on the contacts she had established with the revolutionary unionist milieus of *La Révolution prolétarienne* and of the *Cri du peuple.*

Weil's presence in Le Puy was quite an event. She, a teacher having the rank of *agrégée,* was seen after school shaking the hands of the jobless who were employed temporarily by the mayor's office to break stones in a public square. This same teacher accompanied a delegation to present their demands, then went with them to the café, and, carrying a red flag, marched at the head of their demonstrations—all this did not go unnoticed.

The local press reacted with public indignation. *Le Mémorial* of Saint-Etienne reported: "Mademoiselle Weill (*sic*), a red virgin from the tribe of Levi, messenger of the *moscowtaire* gospel, has indoctrinated the miserable whom she has led astray" (cited in Pétrement, *La Vie,* 179; SWL, 114). Weil gave vent to her anger in a text she published in the bulletin of the Teachers' Union of Haute-Loire. In it she accused the university administration of still laboring under the caste system—"for them there are still untouchables, . . . with whom at any price the parents of the students must never see a professor shaking hands" which led her to demand a "precise ruling to indicate exactly under what conditions and with which members of such and such levels of society each category of the teaching staff has the right to associate" (*La Vie,* 158; SWL, 97). After Le Puy, her professorial career was interrupted by leaves of absence due essentially to very painful headaches. She taught in Auxerre (1932–33), in Roanne (1933–34), then in Bourges (1935–36), and at Saint-Quentin (1937–mid-January 1938).

From as early as 1931, she considered Germany the country where real consideration was given to the problem of a social regime, which in France was the subject of no more than theories and discourses. By leaving for Germany, she made manifest a constant preoccupation in her life: to think and to write in contact with reality. During her stay there she produced four articles, one of which would be developed into a series of ten studies published in the review *L'Ecole émancipée* and later taken up once again in *Ecrits historiques et politiques.* The main lines of her analysis of the German situation brought her to the attention of the leftist milieus. She considered that the constitutive elements of a revolutionary period seemed united in Germany, but that these aspirations would lead nowhere. In her eyes the Nazi party was the "party of reckless and irresponsible revolutionaries" (*Oeuvres complètes* II.1.124), but she did not underestimate its capacity to maintain its position in German politics. She was very skeptical about the capacities of the leftist opposition, judging that the socialist party was bureaucratic and reined in the demands of the workers. The German communist party enjoyed enormous revolutionary prestige, but it was composed essentially of the unemployed, which rendered any infiltration into industry impossible. Reduced to its own particular strengths, Weil judged that this party's power was "nil" and analyzed lucidly the danger of common actions undertaken by the Nazis and the Communists, for example, the transport strike in Berlin. On her return from Germany she confided to a unionist friend that she had lost all respect that she still had for the communist party and judged that for the present "any compromise with [it], any reticence in criticism is criminal" (cited *La Vie,* 212; SWL, 137).

Her German experience joined to that of the situation of the unions and the revolutionary parties in France led Weil to decide in 1934 to "retire completely from any kind of politics." This did not exclude her "eventual participation in a great spontaneous movement of the masses," but she did not want "any responsibility whatsoever," for she said she was sure that any bloodshed would be "in vain, and that they were already defeated" (*La Vie,* 291; SWL, 198).

Her article "Perspectives," published in 1933 in *La Révolution prolétarienne,* clearly explains her change. This article contains some characteristic formulas concerning the USSR, whose regime is like the one "that Lenin thought he was establishing to the extent that he entirely excluded capitalist property; for everything else, he takes the completely opposite position" (*Oeuvres complètes* II.1.262). Against Trotsky she affirms that "the Stalinist regime [must be] considered, not as a worker State gone wrong, but as a different social mechanism, defined by the cogwheels that make it up, and functioning in conformity with the nature of cogwheels." She was equally sensitive to the new forms adopted by capitalism and perceived this as the entry into the era of "management techniques," which the American sociologist James Burnham would name the "managerial revolution" a few years later. Finally she insisted that the crisis of capitalism announced no new regime whatsoever that would in any way resemble socialism as she defined it: "the return to man, that is to say to the individual, the domination that is his proper function to exercise over nature, over tools, over society it-self" (*Oeuvres complètes* II.1.277). She tried to respond to the utter confusion of her era by what she called her "Great Work," *Réflexions sur les causes de la liberté et de l'oppression sociale* (1934), which she set herself to complete before she went to work in a factory.

The dead ends of her reflections on the social question and the dangers of methodical action pushed Simone Weil to become a worker from December 4, 1934 to August 1935.[1] A few months before carrying out her project, she wrote to one of her former students at the lycée of Le Puy saying that she was taking a sabbatical of one year in order to enter into the labor force "and also enter into some contact with that famous 'real life'" (cited in *La Vie*, 319; SWL, 213). This is clear evidence of her desire for truth conceived as contact with reality. If, as she insisted in 1937, "the most important [problem] for the worker movement"—that of the most desirable system for factories—had not been posed by the theorists of socialism, it was because they were "poorly situated to treat this subject, since they themselves had not been numbered among the cogwheels of a factory" (*La Condition ouvrière*, 304).

In the factory Weil came to know a form of extreme hardship, which is why she was able to summarize perfectly the spirit—but also the limits—of the events of June 1936. "As soon as the yoke was loosened, we raised our heads. Period, that's it" (*La Condition ouvrière*, 274). In these events, something other than specific demands came into play; it was about the fact that, after "having always given in, submitted to everything, taken all the hard knocks without saying anything, for months and for years, they finally dared . . . to feel that they were men, for a few days" (275). Consequently, it was the very conditions of work that had to change, and the urgency of this task led her to think about the primary conditions for a "new regime" in the factories.

Just as the days of June 1936 pushed her once again to take part in social action, Simone Weil felt within herself, even though she was a pacifist, the "interior necessity" of leaving for Spain, as she would write to Georges Bernanos in 1938: "When I came to realize that, in spite of my efforts, I could not prevent myself from participating morally in that war, that is to say every day and every hour, to wish for the victory of one group and the defeat of the other, . . . I took the train for Barcelona with the intention of volunteering" (*Oeuvres,* 406; SL, 106). On August 8, 1936 she crossed the frontier and found herself enrolled in a small international company which was involved in carrying out dangerous missions and which was seeking to join the headquarters of the Durruti column.[2] On August 19, as if to confirm her legendary clumsiness and her poor eyesight, she stepped into a basin of boiling oil. This put an end to her enlistment. When she returned to France very pessimistic about the eventual outcome of the Spanish Revolution, she threw herself into the struggle in favor of generalized non-intervention. Although her fellow-combatants in Aragon and later in Catalonia severely condemned the politics of Blum, she approved them, explaining: "This is because I refuse, on my personal responsibility, to deliberately sacrifice the peace, even if there is question of saving a revolutionary people threatened with extermination" (*Oeuvres complètes* II.3.43; FW, 261). Personal engagement is one thing, political decision is entirely another. The choice of nonintervention is heartrending, but she wanted to make it a model for future action: "We will be able to pardon ourselves for having accepted neutrality with regard to the Spanish slaughter only if we do everything in our power to transform this attitude into a precedent that in the future will regulate all French foreign politics" (II.3.282). She also discovered in Spain what leads men to commit monstrosities without becoming monsters, as is shown in her letter to Bernanos: "When temporal and spiritual authorities have put a category of human beings outside those whose lives have a value, there is nothing more natural to man than to kill. . . . Here there is . . . an intoxication that is impossible to resist without a strength of mind that I must certainly believe is exceptional, for I have never encountered this anywhere else" (*Oeuvres,* 408; SL, 108). This experience would nourish her reflection on the roots of barbarism.[3]

In the autumn of 1934 Weil wrote to her friend Albertine Thévenon that she "would retire into her ivory tower" and would leave it only for the struggle against colonial oppression and against anything that would contribute to the preparation for war. Her conscious awakening to the colonial question can be dated to 1930–31 when she read reports on Indochina and the events of the colonial Exposition. Weil's sensitivity to this question came from a feeling of culpability. The feeling that she had participated in a collective transgression aroused in her the need for a personal reparation that could extend even to sacrifice. Apropos the will to humiliate the country conquered by the Treaty of Versailles, she wrote to Bernanos that the humiliations inflicted by her own country were for her "more painful than those that it could suffer" (*Oeuvres,* 409; SL, 109). Her sensitivity to the problem of colonial oppression was such that it transformed even her writing style itself. She became more polemical, ironic, and indignant, whereas in her analysis of social oppression, her writing was more descriptive and conceptual. Take for example her recourse to antiphrasis and to false evidence at the beginning of 1937 in an article on French claims regarding Morocco: "The territory of the nation is threatened . . . Alsace-Lorraine? Yes, precisely. Or rather no, it was not Alsace-Lorraine exactly, but something just like it. It was Morocco . . . that province so essentially French. . . . Germany seemed to be expressing some vague desire to lay its hands on the Moroccan population. . . . Morocco has always been a part of France. Or if not always, at least from a time almost immemorial. . . . To any impartial mind, it is evident that a territory belonging to France since 1911 is rightfully French for all eternity" (*Oeuvres complètes* II.3.123).

In contrast with the common reactions of public opinion, Weil did not attribute the agitation in the colonies and the development of nationalist movements to external causes. In her eyes the

responsible persons were those who treat the indigenous peoples
with disdain, those who "carry out the progressive expropriation of
indigenous farmers, those colonists, industrialists who treat their
workers as beasts of burden, and those functionaries who accept,
demand that, for the same work, they be paid a third more than
their Arab co-workers" (*Oeuvres complètes* II.3.133–34). She admitted that she was ashamed not only of the French democrats and
socialists, but also of the working class, and she deplored the fact
that the official Left refused to recognize the symmetry between
the aspirations of the workers in 1936 and those of the colonized
populations. She never varied on the colonial question, and her
positions influenced even her interpretation of what could be considered a "just war" against Nazism when at the same time democracies themselves were oppressing other peoples.[4]

Pacifism was a long-standing conviction of Simone Weil, dat-
ing back to her years at the Ecole normale. War was not only an
element of foreign politics, but "an episode of internal politics,
and the most atrocious of all" (*Oeuvres complètes* II.1.293), since
it crystallized the relationships of oppression by obliging the individual to sacrifice his very life, and not just wear out his working strength. "Those wars in which slaves are invited to die in the
name of a dignity never accorded them, these wars constitute the
essential cogwheel in the mechanism of oppression" (*Oeuvres complètes* II.2.332).

From 1932 to 1938 Weil's pacifism became firmly attached
to the most extreme positions. So in "L'Europe en guerre pour
la Tchécoslovaquie?" an article published in *Feuilles libres de la
Quinzaine* on May 25, 1938, she showed herself ready for any
compromise to save the peace and to find justifications for the an-
nexation of Sudetenland by Germany. She went so far as to concede
that the Czechs "can outlaw the Communist party and exclude
the Jews from less important functions without losing anything at
all of their national life. In short, injustice for injustice, . . . let us
choose the one which runs the least risk of leading to war" (*Oeuvres*

complètes II.3.82–83). In a letter to Gaston Bergery[5] in April 1938, she made the point that should France permit Hitler to establish his hegemony in Eastern Europe, one could hope that Germany would not take the trouble to invade it. "Without a doubt the superiority of the German forces would lead France to adopt certain restrictions, especially against the communists, against the Jews: this, in my opinion and in that of most Frenchmen, is pretty much a matter of indifference" for "nothing essential would be touched" (*Ecrits historiques et politiques,* 286; SL, 99). It would be useless to look here for a trace of anti-Semitism for it was simply the same strict application of her extreme pacifism that had led Weil to support the politics of non-intervention in Spain[6] by consenting to the crushing of a cause that she held so dear. Only the entry of Hitler's troops into Prague in March 1939 would gradually put an end to the pacifism she regretted having held so long and so obstinately. Notes written in London speak of her "criminal mistake before 1939 about the pacifist milieus and their action"[7] (*Oeuvres complètes* VI.4.374).

Along with her philosophical, social, and political reflections, but on a deeper level, Simone Weil experienced a spiritual change of direction that she steadfastly refused to call a "conversion." After a year in the factories, her parents took the broken young woman suffering from violent headaches to Portugal. In a small village she took part in a procession of fishermen's wives, "who sang hymns of heartbreaking sadness," as she wrote to her Dominican friend Joseph-Marie Perrin, to whom she confessed: "There I had the sudden certitude that Christianity is the religion of slaves, that slaves could not do other than adhere to it, and I along with them" (*Attente de Dieu,* 43; WG, 26). Weil encountered Christianity in the context of a sensitivity to the hardship and slavery that she had lived through in the factories.[8] In 1937, at Assisi, in the little Romanesque chapel of Santa Maria degli Angeli where St Francis had prayed, she recognized that something stronger than herself "obliged her, for the first time in her life, to drop to her knees."

This was her second contact, under the sign of beauty and purity. At Solesmes, during Holy Week in 1938, while she was suffering from intensely painful headaches, she assisted at the divine office sung in Gregorian chant. She said that in the course of these religious services "the thought of the passion of Christ entered into me once and for all" (*Attente de Dieu*, 43; WG, 26). At Solesmes she met a young Englishman who introduced her to the seventeenth-century metaphysical poet George Herbert and gave her the text of his poem *Love*. Toward the end of 1938, several months after her stay at Solesmes, "at the peak of a series of violent headaches" she "set herself to reciting the poem while applying [her] complete attention to it." "I thought I was reciting it simply as some beautiful poem," she wrote to Father Perrin, "but without my awareness that recitation had the force of a prayer. It was in the course of these recitations that . . . Christ himself came down and took possession of me" (*Attente de Dieu*, 44–45; WG, 27). The beauty of the chant, the possibility of loving in the midst of suffering, the felt presence of love during that suffering, these are all elements of this third contact.

These mystical experiences are all inscribed in what Weil called her "particular vocation," which gave her "legitimate reasons" (*Ecrits de Londres*, 205; SL, 172) to take her place at the intersection of what is Christian and what is not. For the moment let us remember simply that she asked herself if, at a time when a "great portion of humanity is submerged in materialism, God does not wish that there be men and women who would give themselves to Him and to Christ and who would dwell outside the Church" (*Attente de Dieu*, 18–19; WG, 6). Likewise she dreaded "the Church as a social entity." If its power was capable of blinding saints, who had given their approval to the Crusades and the Inquisition, "what evil would it not do to me," she wrote, "who am particularly vulnerable to social influences?" (*Attente de Dieu*, 22, 25; WG, 12).

The drive of her vocation led her to make declarations that can appear to be manifestations of pride. Before leaving Marseille for America, she wrote to Father Perrin that "something tells her to leave" and that she abandons herself to it hoping that this abandonment "will lead [her] in the end to a safe harbor." She added that "what I call safe harbor, you know, is the cross. If it cannot be given to me some day to share in the cross of Christ, at least let it be in that of the good thief. . . . To have been at Christ's side and in the same state as in the crucifixion seems to me a much more enviable privilege than to be at His right hand in His glory"[9] (*Attente de Dieu*, 31–32; WG, 18). She understood the pride entailed in desiring the sufferings of Christ, all the while confiding that, each time she thinks of the crucifixion, she "commits the sin of envy" (*Attente de Dieu*, 62; WG, 38). This confession becomes a form of personal repentance, a condition necessary for "decreation," a major term in her spirituality, to which we shall return. "Misfortune without any consolation whatsoever" is one of the "keys by which one enters into the pure land, the land where one can breathe freely, the land of the real," she wrote to Joë Bousquet (*Oeuvres*, 798; SL, 141). She wrote this letter on May 12, 1942, at a time when the war had already deeply upset her life, her thought, and her spiritual progress.

On June 13, 1940, Paris was declared an "open city." Simone's parents left the capital, accompanied by their daughter who accepted this exodus with considerable reluctance for she believed that the French people's duty was to defend themselves, not to flee. By way of Nevers, Vichy, and Toulouse, the Weils arrived in Marseille a little before September 15, 1940. Simone Weil had obtained a sabbatical for health reasons at the beginning of 1938 that had been renewed but was to expire in July 1940. She asked for a post in Algiers, which seemed to her to be the best point of departure for England, not to mention the interest this post held as a point from which to observe the colonial situation. A reply from the ministry appointed her to Constantine, beginning with the opening of the academic year in October 1940, but she never received this letter. Thinking she was a victim of some process of exclusion, she wrote to the Ministry of Public Instruction expressing her surprise at not having received the appointment. She asked if the decree called "Statut des Juifs" [Status of the Jews] applied to her. She insisted that she did not know the definition of the word 'Jew'. If it is a religion, "I have never entered a synagogue," she said. If it is a race, she declared that she had no reason to suppose that she had any relationship whatsoever "with the people who lived in Palestine two thousand years ago" (cited in *La Vie*, 527; SWL, 391). She emphasized the fact that the Christian, French, and Hellenic tradition was hers, and she concluded in the ironic tone that she often used: "If nevertheless the law obliges me to consider the term 'Jew' . . . as an epithet applicable to my person, I am disposed to submit to it as I am to any law whatever it may be. But in this case I want to be officially informed."

In 1940, in the same state of mind as the majority of those who wished to continue the struggle, Weil was convinced that everything depended on England, the last rampart of the democracies threatened by Germany. Her strong belief that England was in danger of having to repel a German invasion led her at the beginning of 1941 to look for a network that would permit her to go to London. Her network was discovered by the police. This led to a house search of the Weils' apartment in May 1941 and to a summons to appear at several interrogations by a commissioner of public safety in Marseille and another to appear before a military tribunal in September.

In Marseille she met the Dominican Joseph-Marie Perrin, with whom she had long conversations about Christianity, the Church, and baptism. Father Perrin put Weil in contact with Gustave Thibon, a farmer and writer, because she wanted to have the experience of working on a farm. She passed two months participating in different forms of agricultural work, including the grape harvest, and she took advantage of this experience in October 1941 to send a letter to Xavier Vallat, Commissioner of Jewish Questions, in which she took up once again the exchange she had with

Commissioner Ripert. In her judgment, the Statut des Juifs was "unjust and absurd," but she did express her "sincere gratitude" to the government for having "removed her from the category of intellectuals" and for offering her instead what the directors themselves did not own, the land and nature, and above all for having bestowed on her "the infinitely precious gift of poverty, which [they certainly] did not [possess] either" (cited in *La Vie,* 591–92; SWL, 444).

On her return from the grape harvest in November 1941, Father Perrin introduced her to Malou David,[10] who distributed the *Cahiers du Témoignage Chrétien* and she had serious responsibility for the distribution of one of the most important clandestine publications in the unoccupied zone. From December 1941 to May 1942 Weil distributed almost 300 copies of each issue and, in league with the resistance activities of the Marseille Dominicans, had false identity papers made up for refugees. This period from September 15, 1940 to May 1942, filled with resistance activities, farm work, and with meetings and work with Father Perrin, was equally rich in writing. Weil frequented the *Cahiers du Sud* for which she wrote several articles. Doing research on the continuity between ancient civilizations, Greek culture, and the Christian message, she composed during this period most of the texts later regrouped in *Intuitions pré-chrétiennes, La Source grecque,* and *Attente de Dieu.* She kept writing in her notebooks, which she gave to Thibon when she left Marseille, and in two articles she returned once again to her work experience in factories.[11]

The Weils sailed for the United States on May 14, 1942. After a long stopover in Casablanca, they arrived in New York, where Simone hoped to obtain passage to join Free France in London. She wrote to several important persons asking for help; among them was Maurice Schumann who had been her fellow-student in Alain's class. André Philip, Commissioner of the Interior in the national committee of Free France, agreed to employ her in services that corresponded to the Ministry of the Interior. On November 9,

1942, she left New York and arrived in Liverpool on the 26th. She had no more than nine months to live.

She did not appreciate the work of an intellectual functionary that she was asked to perform. She did not abandon her desire to be on the front lines, wanting to be parachuted into France to carry out a dangerous mission. She spent much time writing however, for within a few months she produced ten texts later collected in her *Ecrits de Londres*. She also composed *L'Enracinement*, "Y a-t-il une doctrine marxiste?" "A propos de la question coloniale dans ses rapports avec le destin du peuple française," and "Théorie des sacrements," in addition to a notebook and a number of reports that have not yet been published. Among the projects close to her heart was the "formation of frontline nurses," an idea conceived even before the German offensive of 1940 and later attached to a letter addressed to Maurice Schumann.[12] She did not view this project as a simple humanitarian intervention carried out by women ready to sacrifice their lives, but rather as a form of political and strategic action. Hitler understood the importance in war of acting on the imagination through the heroic action of elite troupes made up of men prepared to make the ultimate sacrifice. This led Simone Weil to ask how to create opposition to Hitler by means of *equivalent* procedures that would not be based on a "heroism of brutality." The frontline nurses would make this different orientation of heroism obvious. Present in the areas of the greatest peril, they would bear witness to the "persistence of some good offices of humanity . . . at the highest point of savagery." Small in number, these nurses would be able to care for only a limited number of soldiers, but Weil insisted that "the moral effectiveness of a symbol is independent of its quantity" (*Oeuvres complètes* IV.1.408; SL, 150–51).

Realizing very quickly the difficulty of returning to France, Weil insisted to Schumann that she be given tasks "involving a high degree of effectiveness, of pain, and of danger." "The suffering spread over the surface of this world obsesses me and crushes me to the point of annulling my faculties, and I cannot restore them or free myself from this obsession unless I myself share a large portion of that danger and suffering" (*Ecrits de Londres,* 199; SL, 156). Only by according her permission to share in this could they keep her, she said, from "being sterilely consumed by grief." Adding that this was a "question of vocation," she insisted that her life never had any other meaning than "a waiting for truth," and this is how she defined what she expected at this moment of her life: "I am experiencing a wrenching that never ceases to worsen, both in my intelligence and in the center of my heart, by the incapacity in which I find myself to think in truth, at one and the same time, about the misery of men, the perfection of God, and the link between the two. I have the inner certainty that this truth, if it is ever granted to me, will be only at the moment when, physically, I myself will be . . . in one of the extreme forms of this present suffering" (*Ecrits de Londres,* 213; SL, 178). Jean Cavaillès—whom she met in London—saw in Weil a "case of exceptional nobility, but today we no longer have such an example" he is supposed to have said (cited in *La Vie,* 668; SWL, 515). She was never sent to France.

Her sadness became overwhelming, and she was weakened by the privations she inflicted on herself in order to share the fate of her French compatriots suffering under the constraints of rationing. On April 15, 1943, a friend went to her home and found her stretched out on the floor unable to move. Sent to a hospital in London, then to a sanatorium in Ashford, Simone Weil died on August 24, 1943, eleven days after she was admitted there. Her last letters to her family give no hint about the state of her health. She wrote of insignificant subjects even in her next-to-last letter of August 4, 1943: "Here as dessert we sometimes eat . . . mixtures called *fruit fool.* This is a kind of compote of fruits, strained and mixed with a large quantity . . . of gelatin, or something else" (*Ecrits de Londres,* 255; SL, 200). However, as if she had to express something else without being able to say it brutally, she artificially slipped in subjects that were in some way quite serious:

But these *fools* are not like those of Shakespeare. They lie, pretending they are fruit, whereas in Sh[akespeare] the fools are the only characters who tell the truth. . . .

Do you get a sense of the affinity, the essential analogy between these fools and me—in spite of the Ecole [normale supérieure], the aggregation, the praise of my "intelligence"? . . . A great intelligence is often paradoxical, and at times wanders off a bit into nonsense. . . .

The praise of my [intelligence] had as its *object* to avoid the question: "Is she speaking the truth or not?" My reputation for "intelligence" is the practical equivalent of the fool sign that these fools wear. How much I would prefer their sign!

Maurice Schumann came closest to the truth about Weil's death when he confided: "Reproaching all of us, with a sudden hardness, for not having eliminated the insurmountable obstacle that kept her far from the clandestine struggle, . . . she revealed to us . . . that from now on there was for her only one single conceivable link in truth between the suffering of men and the perfection of God: to let oneself be consumed by grief."[13] A passage from her essay consecrated to the Our Father confirms this interpretation. Apropos the formula that she translates "Our bread, which is supernatural, give it to us today," Weil comments: "If our energy is not renewed daily, we lose our strength and become unable to move. Outside what is properly called nourishment, in the literal sense of the word, all stimulants are sources of energy for us. . . . If one of these stimulants penetrates profoundly within us, to the very vital roots of our carnal existence, its deprivation can break us and even cause us to die. This is called dying of grief. It is like dying of hunger" (*Oeuvres completes* IV.1.341; WG, 147).

At the end of her life, Simone Weil still had the strength to hope, as she wrote poignantly to Maurice Schumann: "I desire nothing for myself except to be in the number of those who are not forbidden to think of themselves as useless slaves, having done only what they were commanded to do" (*Ecrits de Londres*, 211; SL, 176). Simone Pétrement gave the most beautiful commentary on this slavery, considered as obedience and not as submission to constraint, which reveals the meaning of the death of her friend, whom "grief rendered indifferent in great measure to whatever could happen to her":

> Nevertheless it seems probable to me that we should not speak of indifference [with regard to her recovery], but rather of obedience. . . . She had become, it seems, truly incapable of nourishing herself normally. Nothing else remained for her except to carry out the "supreme act of total obedience," that is to say, her consent to die. Until that point, she perhaps did nothing other than remain obstinately faithful to what she regarded as an obligation, an order. She accepted the risk that this fidelity brought with it, but there is nothing to prove that she had in mind anything other than this very fidelity. (*La Vie*, 682; SWL, 528)

chapter two

The Exercise of
Philosophical Thought

For Simone Weil the beginning of philosophy is an awakening to the real. She traced the line of her philosophical itinerary:

> We exist in unreality, in a dream. To renounce our central imaginary situation, to abandon it not only by our intelligence, but also in the imaginative part of the soul, is to wake up to the real, to the eternal, to see the true light, to hear the true silence. A transformation takes place at the very root of sensitivity . . . a transformation analogous to that which takes place when in the evening, along some road, at a spot where we thought we noticed a crouching man, we suddenly discern a tree; or when, believing we heard a whisper, we find out it was a rustling of leaves. We see the same colors, we hear the same sounds, but not in the same way." (*Oeuvres complètes* IV.1.300; WG, 100)

Spiritual preoccupations certainly nourished this text written in 1942. We must renounce the illusion of being the center of the world if we wish to discern "the true center as being outside this world." Her first writings as a student in 1929 already concluded this from related examples that permitted her, in her own words, to "conceive what could be for me the changes of a world, which leaves an impression on me only through the intermediary of the imagination" (*Oeuvres complètes* I, 122). From her work with Alain, she retained the initial active role of the imagination, so that the image we have of this world "does not reflect itself alone, it also reflects us to ourselves" (I, 298). From the ambiguity of the limits between the self and the world and of the initial condition of man immersed in this world like a wave in the ocean—which she calls the "reign of Proteus"[1]—arise the first degrees of knowledge in relation to the levels of being by means of a redrafting of the "divided line" of *The Republic*.[2] From the half-awakened spirit we pass to the dream, that "perception which is based on insufficient data" according to Alain. Next, the spirit "demands an account of what it sees" (I, 131), but it becomes conscious of its idealism, the infantile state in which the world, as interpreted, is never encountered. The spirit will clothe these impressions "with ideas" (I, 123), organizing the qualities and forms perceived. However, this knowledge remains mixed with beliefs that correspond to the emotional attachments of the body. What remains to be done is to purify the appearance of every mixture of emotion and illusion, going as far back as the "Cartesian clairvoyance," which makes it permissible to posit extension as the "substance of each thing" (I, 134), and to think of the world under the idea of exteriority. Yet it is difficult to constantly maintain this Cartesian point of view, and it is useless without an art of perception capable of freeing us from credulity without reflection on geometry. The development of such an art is necessary to save us from the "reign of Proteus," at the same time freeing us from having to remain permanently at the level of pure extension. We need an exercise regulated by the union of spirit and body, a gymnastics accompanied by art, formative of "privileged perceptions" (I, 137) which help us learn to discipline our emotions.

We end up with an athlete's body and a geometrician's mind, something Plato would not have denied, but like Plato we have expressed only the half of it. We have bodily activity and perception; we have the necessity conceived by geometry and science, but to be fully in the world, we lack the "*test*" of real necessity. From this lack comes the obligation to go all the way to the concept of work. The law that makes work of all our actions is neither "imagined, nor supposed, nor proven, but perpetually experienced" (I, 126). This law imposes on our projected actions "the conditions established . . . by the universe for its own changes" (I, 155), and this is called 'work'. The formative activity by which we move from the first impression to the object in the world is not the judgment, nor the imaginative synthesis, nor the Kantian schema; it is work, which thus becomes the true schema for Simone Weil.[3] According to her, it is not only the object that is represented, imagined, under the form of an expectation of the affections of which it would be the source if we touched it—this was Alain's interpretation. The imagination renders "the law of working" particularly perceptible by means of mimed movements.[4] More precisely, it makes perceptible the geometric law that, in itself, expresses the law of work. The worker is the one who, by working in accordance with the necessities of geometry, *experiences* the truth of the conceived necessities. In this he experiences real necessity.

Such is the Platonism worked out by Weil in her first writings, in which work is envisaged as the activity that leads us to discover the form of the human condition. She did not hold to a philosophy of perception, to a phenomenology of "the directed toward," rather she preferred a "dynamology of contradiction,"[5] an exercise of our properly equipped capacity to penetrate the exteriority and to cause our presence in the world to be experienced in a relationship of work.

Going Beyond the Philosophers at the Very Center of Their Thought[6]

Independently of her social commitment, Simone Weil was destined to encounter Marx, who showed that reality becomes apparent in a *praxis* "at the contact of thought and the world"[7] (*Oeuvres complètes* II.1.306; OL, 33). If work is the human activity *par excellence,* it is because it is first and foremost a thought that must be interpreted as a disposition to act. When Weil affirms that "the philosophy of work is *materialism,*" it is to state clearly from the first that "materialism is inconceivable without the notion of spirit" (*Oeuvres complètes* I, 378–79). Matter and its inevitable order dictate the "necessary gesture," and consequently "everything is matter except the thought that grasps necessity." Thus is avoided the idealist interpretation, which would be thought exercised without any contact with real necessity: "There is no question at all of thinking and working; work is no less a thought than is reflection. It is no less an absolute act of the spirit." In this sense, the thought of Marx is a philosophy defined as the only study "in which the condition is always to begin with the subject, as long as it is not forgotten that the subject is empirically determined."[8] Thus understood, Marx is inscribed in that line of philosophers who, by their method, come from the Platonism of Descartes and Kant (*Oeuvres complètes* IV.1.67).

Yet Weil judged that these philosophers were not sufficiently conscious of their method of investigation, which was to their disadvantage. If "Plato expressed only the half of it," Descartes "said explicitly what Plato only hinted at" (*Oeuvres complètes* I, 133), pushing ahead to the idea of a geometry turned toward the world (I, 96). "Descartes stopped halfway," however (*Oeuvres complètes* II.2.270); he perceived that the question of signs was essential for thought, but he did not keep the signs from taking the place of the signified and becoming their own end, as is the case in algebra.[9] He did not discover the means to understand without ceasing to perceive.[10] Kant was the first to reveal the link between understanding and intuition by making this apparent in its real exercise, but he should have brought in more perceptibly the important role of the body on the outward aspect of existence through work. Maine de Biran went further by making effort "the real in perception," but he did not go so far as to consider the real as "contradiction experienced through work" (*Oeuvres complètes* VI.3.64). As for Marx, after having discovered the explanation of the historical process in the relationships produced by the activity of individuals, he hypostatized the real conditions of that activity into an essence that realizes itself. He betrayed his philosophy of the subject when he claimed that "social existence determines conscience," as if social existence were separate from the conscience of the individual who acts. In the end, Alain recognized that "a philosophy of work was still in its embryonic stage,"[11] but his "view of mechanization was too superficial and simplistic" to elaborate it properly, as Simone tells us in the *Journal d'usine* (*La Condition ouvrière*, 189). A continuation of the philosophical tradition definitely has to pass through a philosophy of work, which moreover is a "need of this present epoch" (*Oppression et liberté*, 223; OL, 169).

The place attributed to work then is philosophically constitutive of an analysis of knowledge.[12] How, at this time, can the awakening to the real, the philosophy of work, and social criticism be put together? By acknowledging the fact that the value of the working toward a purified knowledge of the real is impeded by the opacity of the social form of production. What Weil calls "oppression" is first of all the reality of a social organization of work that hinders the individual from experiencing in a complete fashion his presence in the world through the exercise of all his faculties. The present form of factory work prohibits the renewal of "the original pact between the spirit and the universe" (*Oeuvres complètes* II.2.109; OL, 124). This idea runs through all her writing. In 1930, when she wrote that "the workers know everything" (*Oeuvres complètes* I, 217), but that their oppression kept them from discovering that they knew everything, Weil announced what she would take up again at another level in 1942: nothing separates the workers from God, but it is "difficult for them to raise their heads" because the conditions of industrial work destroy the exercise of attention to the supernatural.[13]

The Philosophy of Work and Social Critique

Her *Réflexions sur les causes de la liberté et de l'oppression sociale* (1934) sketched out a criticism of Marxism on the basis of the contradiction that undermines our societies. This contradiction is found not between the productive forces and the relationships of production that would hamper their development, but rather between the development of the productive forces and the material conditions of production. Weil returned to a thesis of the Austrian Marxist Julius Dickman,[14] who tried to show that the struggle for power never fails to transform the conditions of production by pushing for development, all the while diminishing the material base, natural resources, and sources of energy. As soon as the quest for power exceeds the limits imposed by natural conditions, it "extends beyond what it is able to control" and engenders growing waste, and finally oppression. "Capitalism certainly seems to be going through a phase of this kind" (*Oeuvres complètes* II.2.65; OL, 76).

On this basis the social question must be redefined in order to ask ourselves "if it is possible to conceive of an organization of production which, even though incapable of eliminating natural necessities and their resulting social restraint, would at least permit them to be carried out without crushing both spirits and bodies under oppression" (*Oeuvres complètes* II.2.46; OL, 56). Note that the social question is conceived as one about the organization of production and not as one about the form of government or about the form of property. Weil never deviated from the objective of social transformation as she defined it in 1932: "To re-establish the control of the worker over the conditions of work, without destroying the collective form that capitalism has imprinted on production" (*Oeuvres complètes* II.2.94).

She marks her originality regarding Marx by distinguishing oppression—the phenomenon of domination by those who command over those who carry out the commands—from exploitation, which plays an essential role in the capitalist economy as such. The new forms of oppression stemming from the historic transformation of the capitalist mechanism of exploitation have in fact provoked a new form of class division. If in the days of workshops and factories money alone divided the industrial population in two, "in the days of huge industries, it is the machine itself that separates . . . on the one hand those who direct, and on the other those who form the cogwheels" of those industries (*Oppression et liberté*, 260). Consequently, the two classes were no longer "those who sell and those who buy the workforce, but those who dispose of the machine and those of whom the machine disposes" (261). The result is a complete transformation of the social question, for if one could conceive of a revolution that would suppress money or change its function, it is difficult to see "how the social properties of mechanization could be transformed."

A Reading of the Contradictions in Marx

For Marx a revolution takes place at the moment when it is already almost carried out. "That part of society to which the revolution gives power is that part which, even before the revolution began, and even though victimized by institutions, actually played the most active role" (*Oeuvres complètes* II.2.136; OL, 148). Marx got his strange notion of revolution by supposing that, despite "everything being controlled by force," a proletariat without any force was going to seize power, suppress private property by juridical means, "and find itself the master of all the domains of social life" (*Oppression et liberté*, 212; OL, 162). This supposition is as contrary as it could possibly be to his very own principles, since he has shown how in the industrial world the abyss between manual work and intellectual work has relegated the mind of the worker to the level of objects without value and how manual dexterity itself has been taken away from men. At the same time he wanted to believe that, while everything remained intact, the proletariat would free itself and exercise command. On the contrary, Weil thought that everything that causes the oppression and enslavement of the proletariat had to disappear *before* a revolution takes place, otherwise "it would be nothing more than an apparent revolution, which would leave the oppression intact or even aggravate it" (*Oeuvres complètes* II.2.137; OL, 150).

A capitalist society does not produce the material conditions for a regime of freedom and equality. The role of the proletariat as producer of merchandise in no way signifies its dominant role in the factory, in the social order, or in the technique of work and of the administration of men and things. In 1943 Weil was still astonished at the supposition according to which "a day will come suddenly when force would be on the side of the weak. Not that some of the weak would become strong . . . but that the entire mass of the weak, while remaining the mass of the weak, would have force on its side" (*Oppression et liberté*, 252; OL, 193). For coherence sake, it must be recognized that a revolution, should it take place, would be the consecration of a transformation already carried out by social forces playing a dominant role ahead of time in the social order.

Though he considered that necessity and force ruled history, Marx wanted to conceive of a just society that would escape from necessity while still being a product of history. He found himself face to face with the difficulty of scientifically understanding a necessity powerful enough to hinder men from obtaining justice or from even conceiving of it, and still not abandoning hope for a just world. The only thing left for him was to take refuge "in a dream in which social matter itself carries out the two functions that it forbids to man, that is, not only to bring about justice, but even to think of it" (*Oppression et liberté,* 248; OL, 190). In this position Weil saw an abandonment of thought.

In line with her criticism of Marxism, she took issue with contemporary social projects that she considered illusory. Thus she rejected every model of a dualist society in which all socially necessary and enslaving work would be reduced, leaving room for extended periods of leisure.[15] Nothing would be gained by an excessive reduction of the workday due to the development of productivity while conserving a social organization based on the opposition between a sphere of necessity and a sphere of freedom, in which she felt that individuals would be given over to their passions or to consumerism. The automation of production, that is, shifting necessity to the side of machines, and of objective systems of coordination would lead to living in a magical world, delivering the spirit over to fantasy and to confrontation with the wishes of others.

The ideal solution would be in the just combining of freedom with necessity. This is suggested by a note in her notebooks commenting on this formula of Marx: "Ideal: 'From the reign of necessity to the reign of freedom'.[16] No, but necessity subjected to a well-handled necessity" (*Oeuvres complètes* VI.1.91). The freest of societies, whether socialist or otherwise, would be "a form of material life in which there would be a question only of efforts exclusively directed by clear thought, which would imply, without reference to any exterior regulation, that each worker himself would control the adaptation of his efforts to the work to be produced, but also their coordination with the efforts of all the other members of the collectivity" (*Oeuvres complètes* II.2.85; OL, 98–99).

Having pushed as far as possible her theoretical reflection on the ideal limit of all realizable social transformation, all that remained for Weil to do to go beyond the theoreticians of the worker movement was to conduct a personal testing of "real life" under oppression.

A Philosopher of the Working Class

In the factory where she was hired in 1938, Simone Weil discovered the negation of the human condition and of the "needs of the soul," an idea so essential to *L'Enracinement* (1943). In her *Journal d'usine* she wrote down her "impressions" of what was most difficult to understand and express: the misery that "creates a zone of silence in which human beings find themselves imprisoned as if on a desert island" (*La Condition ouvrière*, 342). Throughout her journal, Weil describes in detail not only her fatigue but also her nausea, her sense of being a slave. She reveals her tears, her hunger, and that "wave of anger and bitterness, which in the course of such an existence she experiences constantly in her deepest self" (*La Condition ouvrière*, 164; FW, 221), the fear, the harsh reprimands, the worry about falling asleep and waking up right away, the repression of her capacity to think. The body suffers, of course, but the capital fact is the humiliation. On leaving the factory, the body is worn out, but the mind even more so, to the point that on entering "one would prefer to lay down one's soul along with one's time card and reclaim it intact on leaving!" (*La Condition ouvrière*, 335; SWR, 59).

Enslavement in the factory, in fact, is not in the circumstances nor in the juridical status; it is in the work itself: monotony, rapidity, time being ceaselessly at the disposition of the bosses. Slavery is written into the way work is organized, that is to say, the foreman in the factory is the master of space and especially of time. The cadence brings about the imprisonment of body and of spirit in a point of space and above all in a repeated identical instant with nothing to mark when "one thing has finished and another is beginning" (*La Condition ouvrière*, 337; SWR, 61). This is why the factory is compared to the reign of Proteus, the mysterious reign of metamorphoses described in her early writings as hindering the formation of ideas of space and time. Work should free us from metamorphosis by making us experience the world as controllable exteriority. So the factory establishes a situation in which the body and spirit are exiles, given over to a monotony broken only by an incident on the machine or by the brutality of an order that entails a change of activity. One then has to become a "machine of flesh" (*La Condition ouvrière*, 358) and nevertheless remain vigilant. The worker is handed over to the most contradictory demands and impressions since he has to "become a thing that has no permission to lose consciousness" (*La Condition ouvrière*, 337; SWR, 60). It is not surprising that the *Journal d'usine* gives this definition of misery: "What count in human life are not the events that dominate in the passing years—or even the months—or even the days. It is the way in which one minute is linked to the following one. And what this costs for each one in body, in soul—and above all in the exercise of the faculty of attention—to bring about and maintain this linkage minute by minute" (*La Condition ouvrière*, 186–87).

In an entirely different context, a passage in "L'*Iliade* ou le poème de la force" describes this crushing force: "There are miserable . . . beings who, without dying, turn into things for their whole lives. In the course of their workdays there is no moment of leisure, no empty time, no free area for anything that comes from themselves. . . . This thing aspires at every moment to be a man, a woman, and at no moment succeeds" (*Oeuvres complètes* II.3.231; SWR, 157–58). For Weil herself, the rough contact with real life, which she nevertheless sought, meant that all the reasons on which the sense of dignity, the respect for oneself are based, "were radically shattered in two or three weeks under the blow of brutal and daily constraint." All of this aroused in her what she expected the least: "The docility of a resigned beast of burden" (*La Condition ouvrière*, 59; SL, 22).

As for the political consequences of oppression, they are formidable. Weil encountered in the factory the very opposite of those skilled workers who carried over into social action their strength of soul and their methodical spirit. The worker enslaved to the machine, whose only stimulants are fear and money, is incapable of transposing something of his work outside the sphere of work. Humiliation and the loss of identity push him to seek compensation in political life as well as in private life. In political life such compensation is called "worker imperialism," that "limitless pride: of the oppressed, provoked by the thought that "his class is destined to make history and dominate everything" (*La Condition ouvrière,* 351; SWR, 71). The society of slave workers creates the conditions for all forms of totalitarianism, that of communism which flatters the imperialism of the workers and that of fascism which flatters the anti-capitalism of the masses. The conclusion of this experience is easily drawn: "Much evil has come from factories; this evil in the factories must be corrected."

The Science of Machines against Scientific Organization of Work

After several months of work, Simone Weil's reflections on social and political matters seemed to take on a reformist direction as compared with the revolutionary direction of her early years. Above all she asked what could be done in the actual conditions to establish a new internal industrial regime, and she replied that all that could be done for the time being "is to look for the most human organization compatible with a given level of production" (*La Condition ouvrière,* 210). The ties that Weil developed with new negotiators—owner (Auguste Detoeuf, founder of Alsthom), technical director of the factory (Victor Bernard, at the Rosières factory), engineer (Jacques Lafitte)—do not signify that she aligned herself with a position of class collaboration. Her attitude at the time of the outbreak of the 1936 strikes is proof enough.[17] Judging that a technical revolution that would bring about "the perception of man at work" (*Sur la science,* 112) at the center of social life was a prerequisite for any political transformation, she felt constrained to seek out, along with specialists, solutions to advance from a rationalization of work to a science of machines. This would furnish a glimpse of a superior form of work that was both mechanical and free.

On this point, her reflection on immediate measures joined her analysis of the causes of oppression. Coordination, necessary for social life, becomes oppression, she wrote in a letter to Robert Guihéneuf in 1936 (*Cahiers Simone Weil* [March-June, 1998]: 15), when human activities become "through specialization, so impenetrable to each other, and . . . entangled in so complicated a manner" that the only possibility is to entrust coordination to signs and to things. Men themselves "become strangers and impenetrable to one another" (*Oeuvres complètes* II.2.86; OL, 99). Their relations are organized completely from the outside; they become perfectly foreign to any individual spirit, even to that of the foreman. Oppression insists on the exteriorization of a process that imitates the spirit while being completely foreign to it. In machines, for example, the "method is so perfectly crystallized in metal that they seem to be the ones who do the thinking" (*Oeuvres complètes* II.2.97; OL, 92). There is a parallelism between the transformation of science (by signs), that of work (by machines), and that of the social (by money, bureaucracy, and totalitarianism). These are three aspects of the same dispossession of the thinking individual: "Money, mechanization, algebra, the three monsters of contemporary civilization. The analogy is complete," as she sums up in her notebook (*Oeuvres complètes* VI.1.100).

Simone Weil's critique could not go forward without a deeper reflection on rationalization. Rationalization requires an organization of work based on "the scientific utilization of living matter, that is to say of men" (*La Condition ouvrière,* 303). This "second industrial revolution" expected from Taylorism a greater economic efficiency through control of the rhythm of work. In addition, Taylorism expected from its method the suppression of class struggle, since its system relied "on a common interest of the worker and the owner, both of them gaining more, and the consumer himself being satisfied because the products would be cheaper" (*La Condition ouvrière*, 319). Weil carefully examined this aspect of the Taylor doctrine, for she knew only too well what class collaboration and what anesthesia for social conflicts could be established on such bases.[18] She dreaded the full adaptation of Taylorism to the structure of large industries, which would increase the risk of seeing oppression maintained independently of the capitalist form of exploitation. Coherent with her analysis of the shifting of the class contradiction was her understanding that Taylorism is more a doctrine of an engineer than of a capitalist. This would favor its implantation in a juridical and political context and abolish the private ownership of the means of production.

It was necessary, precisely, to replace this degraded method by a true science that would be neither a science of work nor a psychotechnology seeking better conditions for the worker while keeping the existing machines in factories such as they were. The last pages of the *Journal d'usine* return to a project sketched out in 1930: "To search for the *material* conditions of clear thought" (*La Condition ouvrière*, 190). After having discovered by her philosophical path that work is the formative activity of our relationship to the real, Weil felt the need, based on her experience as a worker, to come back to the question of the conditions necessary for the exercise of understanding in labor activity. What was needed was a "*new method of reasoning* that was absolutely *pure* and at the same time intuitive and concrete" (*La Condition ouvrière,* 189). The search for such a method has one single purpose, "to get a glimpse of a technical transformation that opens the way to another civilization"[19] (*Oeuvres complètes* VI.1.112), and why not a "civilization founded on the spirituality of work."

chapter three

On the Good Use
of Materialism

"The contemporary form of authentic grandeur," wrote Simone
Weil, "is a civilization organized by a philosophy of work. . . .
But only with trembling can one touch such an expression. How
to touch it without soiling it?" (*L'Enracinement,*127; NR, 97).
The question of the spirituality of work is matched with a more
general difficulty: incomprehensible solutions must not be offered for problems that evade human faculties, in particular the
problem of the unity between the good and necessity.[1] However,
among the insufficient solutions proposed, certain ones "contain
fragments of pure truth" (*Oppression et liberté,* 232; OL, 177),
and curiously such is the case, at first approach, with "materialist solutions." From this point of view, the writings of Marx
contain precious instructions that he distorted by indeterminate
syntheses with the ideal of justice or of the good. Marx had set
out to be such a materialist by introducing into social science
the notion of "conditions of existence" applied by Darwin to the

structures and the transformation of living beings.[2] Nevertheless, his theory of the unlimited development of productive forces capable of automatically creating the structures best adapted to their growth shows that Marx is more closely related to Lamarck than to Darwin. By introducing an aspiration toward the good into social necessity, which is woven of forces, Marx transformed the materialist approach into a mythology. Only a materialism capable of putting aside all concern for the good would be perfectly coherent.

At all the stages of her thought, Weil held that one has to be a materialist in the study of necessity. Materialism "takes account of everything except the supernatural," she wrote in 1943 (*Oppression et liberté*, 232; OL, 177). From 1934 on, she maintained that "all can be explained by matter, except thought itself which grasps and understands the role of matter" (*Oeuvres complètes* II.1.353). The universe here below is nothing but matter; this is the reason why its description must not be distorted by combining matter with "specifically moral forces supposedly belonging to this world" (*Oppression et liberté*, 232; OL, 177), but which come only through the spirit.

From the materialist conception that can and should explain everything except the spirit that understands and transforms the world to the conception of a materialism that can and should explain everything except the supernatural that operates decisively but secretly, Weil crossed a threshold, even though the direction of her thought did not change. Authentic spirituality, far from forcing true materialism to draw back, makes us understand that the "compact, inalterable fragments of truth [which are] infinitely precious" (*Oppression et liberté*, 225; OL, 170) in Marx's thought, for example, are fragments of pure materialism. Marx gave special consideration to "social matter," but it is possible under certain conditions, and by avoiding all simplistic materialism, to understand the use of the notion of a "non-physical matter": "Under all the phenomena of the moral order, whether collective or individual, there is something analogous to matter as such. Something analogous; yet not matter itself."

Under the notion of matter we find developed, as much as it can be, the notion of real necessity. In her first writings, Weil affirmed that "the real and necessity are one and the same thing" (*Oeuvres complètes* I, 376). A fragment from 1943 confirms that "all that is real is subject to necessity" (*Oppression et liberté*, 234; OL, 178). Only by being a materialist to the fullest extent can one put the notion of value in its proper place, as is proved by Weil's considerations on progress.

The Limits of Human Progress

Our so-called scientific culture has given us the habit of "arbitrarily extrapolating, instead of studying the conditions of a phenomenon and the limits they imply" (*Oeuvres complètes* II.2.38; OL, 47). Marx fell into this error by putting dialectics at the service of a metaphysics of endless becoming. Weil aimed her criticism essentially at the Marxist thesis of the unlimited development of productive forces. To suppose such a development would imply "a limitless increase in the productivity of work," whose principle would remain just as inexplicable for him. The study of the conditions of a phenomenon and of the limits they imply should correspond to the progress Darwin brought about with respect to Lamarck. Weil wished to bring about this progress with respect to Marx.

According to Marx, the hypothesis of an unlimited growth of the output from work rests on the idea that it is the connections with capitalist production that shackle the development of productive forces. The task of a revolution would essentially consist in the emancipation of these forces by abolishing private ownership of the means of production, which in turn would result in the emancipation of the workers. Applying to history all that Kant said about metaphysical questions, Weil established the idea that the notion of a limited development of productive forces is not fixed by the boundaries of our reason, "but by those of experience, which contain the givens necessary for reason."[3] To the belief in the simultaneous development of technique and of human freedom by the simple fact of a reversal of juridical and economic obstacles (private property and exploitation), she opposed the very real element of the conditions of social existence, that which produces and reproduces those conditions, namely work. Instead of a calculation based on the illusion of an unlimited development of productive forces, the practice of some form of real compatibility would be necessary. This would come down to asking what forms of work would imply the complete reorganization of the apparatus of production in order to adapt it to its new end, the well-being of the masses, and from what burden of labors could men be freed by carrying out a revolution that would proceed to the expropriation of the capitalists.

Within these limits, Weil examined the notion of technical progress by distinguishing the procedures available to produce more with less effort. Without contesting the possibility of utilizing new energies in the future, she reasoned in terms of economizing, spending, or wasting work. The process of the rationalization of work in space, the economic factors of which are the concentration, division, and coordination of the work, would necessarily attain "the limit after which the technical progress must inevitably be transformed into a factor of economic regression," without our being able to know if we are close to or far from that limit. In addition it is quite possible that the limit be reached and overshot.[4] This does not mean that history has come to a standstill, but rather that the axis of the social system is "in the process of turning over." During the rise of the industrial regime social life was oriented toward construction; at present, the struggle for economic power pushes on toward conquest, and since "conquest is destructive, the capitalist system . . . is oriented entirely toward destruction"

(*Oeuvres complètes* II.2.100; OL, 115). This explains the importance of war in the problematic of Simone Weil.[5]

Finally there is another dimension of rationalization, that of the coordination of efforts in time, "the most important factor in technical progress" (*Oeuvres complètes* II.2.41; OL, 50): "Since Marx, it is customary to designate it by speaking of the substitution of dead work for living work, a formula of frightful imprecision, in the sense that it evokes the image of a continuous evolution toward a stage of technology in which, if it can be expressed this way, all the mental effort of work to be done would have already been done." This is the fanciful hope of a complete automation of production, analogous to an immediately and permanently accessible source of energy with no additional consumption of energy. Such an automated system would brutally accelerate economic temporality, and this acceleration would encounter geological temporality stored in the reserves of raw materials and in the sources of energy, which growth consumes as if they were inexhaustible. At the risk of becoming more costly in human efforts to exploit raw materials and energy, automation would add the danger of rapidly exhausting those resources. Finally, Weil notes, since automatic machines have no advantages other than producing in series and in massive quantities, their use would accelerate the "temptation to produce much more than is necessary to satisfy real needs" (*Oeuvres complètes* II.2.43; OL, 53).

From 1934 on, in a very original way, Weil pinpointed the consequences of joining together the illusion of the revolutionary development of mechanization with ignorance, in the economic domain, of the scientific analyses of energy and entropy, the worst consequence of that ignorance being the "mad idea that work could one day become superfluous."

In Marx, such a utopia would correspond to a historic eschatology according to which the real course of history could become a "paradise-producing mechanism" (*Oppression et liberté*, 207; OL, 158). This historic eschatology draws from the spring of a cosmic eschatology, which ends up by "considering matter as a machine to fabricate good" (*Oppression et liberté*, 228; OL, 173). Weil explains this confusion of levels by the use Marx made of Hegel's dialectic.[6] While attributing an activity to the spirit alone, Hegel already saw this "hidden spirit at work in the universe" (*Oeuvres complètes* II.2.35; OL, 44). Under the name of "Spirit of the world," God again appeared "as the motor of history" (*Oppression et liberté*, 175; OL, 132). Feuerbach pointed out very clearly the idea that history is the work of man, but without explaining how a "juxtaposition of men considered only as natural beings" can bring about "a regular and ascendant development of humanity." Marx's discovery was to use Hegel's dialectic movement, while having this movement rise from a material process, in the worldegel's dialectid movement-while having Hegel's dialecticegel alreade in order to "surmount the isolated 'human being' of Feuerbach." Marx returned to this Hegelian spirit, mixing it in with "social material" and trying to change necessity into freedom. The reversal by which he pretended "to put [Hegelian dialectic] back on its feet" permitted him to attribute only to matter aspirations that are those of the spirit by means of "dialectical materialism."

Despite everything, the contradictions in Marx are not the sign of the less valid aspect of his work, for the contradictions that the spirit runs up against far from always being "a criterion of error [are] sometimes a sign of truth" (*Oppression et liberté*, 228; OL, 173), a "criterion of the real."[7] In this case, the fundamental philosophical contradiction in the thought of Marx points out clearly the essential contradiction of the human condition: "Man having as his very essence the effort toward the good is at the same time subject . . . to a necessity absolutely indifferent to the good." Marx gave proof of his genius by foreseeing that each act of our will "is contradictory to the conditions or consequences attached to it" (*Oeuvres complètes* VI.3.96). With Marx, however, this idea remained sterile.

The Spiritual Point of View

We are never materialist enough when we want to study reality. Curiously, this is a lesson from Weil's writings during a period in which spiritual preoccupations dominated her thought. Moral phenomena themselves are subject to a specific necessity, to a "moral heaviness that continually drags [the human condition] downward" (*Oppression et liberté*, 218; OL, 166). In the study of this heaviness, "one cannot be too cold, too lucid, too cynical. In this sense . . . one must be a materialist." Even the role of the supernatural here below, in its silent intervention, does not escape from the law of the real, which is necessity. To deny that this intervention can be studied as a specific form of necessity is to deny the *reality* of the supernatural: "True knowledge of the social mechanism implies the knowledge of the conditions under which the supernatural operation of an infinitely small quantity of pure good, when properly placed, can neutralize this heaviness." The distance that separates the spirituality of Plato from materialism, in this sense, appears "infinitely small" (*Oppression et liberté*, 230; OL, 174) because between true materialism and authentic spirituality, there is no real contradiction; there is only a paradox for the human intelligence that struggles to recognize the role of the supernatural here below.

chapter four

Philosophy
and Spirituality

Simone Weil was reared in an environment of complete agnosticism.
During her adolescence she became interested in the religious aspect of existence, but until she experienced an absolutely unexpected live contact with Christ, she followed her first conviction
according to which the "problem of God is a problem of which
certain givens are missing here below and the only certain method
to avoid solving it falsely . . . is not to pose it at all" (*Attente de
Dieu*, 36–37; WG, 22). Indeed she states clearly: "While the name
of God played no role in my thoughts with regard to the problems of this world and the Christian conception of this life, such
thoughts did play a role in an explicit, rigorous manner with the
most specific notions that it involves." This conception with regard
to the problems of this world expresses on another level what Weil
called "implicit faith" (*Attente de Dieu*, 75; WG, 47). "Implicit
faith" is the fact that, without the name of God being part of the
slightest thought, without there being the slightest effort to break

out of agnosticism or atheism, the supernatural acts within the soul and Christian virtues animate existence. "Implicit faith" includes the possibility of the supernatural efficacy of a virtue which may not be explicitly Christian, Stoic virtue, for example. "Implicit love," which can "attain very high levels of purity and strength," is a gift—made to an individual "in secret"—which permits him to give. It is not the love of man for God that is implicit, it is the love of God for the man who gives without knowing that it is God, within him, who gives. Also, "whoever loves his neighbor as himself, even if he denies the existence of God, loves God" without knowing it (*Oeuvres complètes* VI.2.390). The word 'implicit' designates the distance between the hastening of God into a soul attentive to those who suffer and the time that the soul takes to become conscious of this presence.

Elements of Mysticism

In the case of Simone Weil, only the contact with something stronger than herself led her to cross the threshold of explicit faith. God came to "seize her soul while suppressing her senses" (*Oeuvres complètes* VI.3.136; SWR, 487); so the very name of God imposed itself on her.[1] If there had been a preparatory period of waiting and desire, it was desire and waiting in a vacuum. At that time the soul could not know if something offered a real response to its love: "It can believe that it knows this. But believing is not knowing. . . . The soul knows only that it suffers hunger," and the most important thing is "that it cry out its hunger," like a child who does not cease crying out even "if he is told that perhaps there is no bread" (*Oeuvres complètes* IV.1.334; SWR, 487). For the danger is not that the soul doubts the existence of the bread, "but that it becomes persuaded that it suffers no hunger"; this would be a lie, for "the reality of its hunger is not a belief, it is a certitude."

A comparison with beauty can help us understand what it means for the soul to "love in a vacuum." The beauty of the world arouses in us the feeling of the presence of a finality—of the *form* of a finality—but any particular idea of this finality is absent from our representation of it. This feeling frees desire from any particular inclination of the self.[2] It would be an error to believe that if an aesthetic judgment is without an object there would be nothing real about our desire for beauty. So attention to beauty, attention in a vacuum, is a manifestation of the reality of the aesthetic sentiment as an opening toward a supreme absence. This sheds light on what suffering hunger can mean for the soul.[3] This absence "arouses hunger, but there is no nourishment in it for that part of the soul which tries to satisfy that hunger here below; there is nourishment only for that part of the soul which gazes" (*Ecrits de Londres,* 37; SWR, 333). Hunger promises without giving, arouses desire by creating "the impression that there is nothing to desire, for we insist above all that nothing about it change." The desire for nothing, for this supreme absence, this is the desire for God, who alone has the power to make Himself known.

When she lived a "real contact, of person to person, here below, between a human being and God" (*Attente de Dieu,* 45; WG, 27), Weil described this experience as the sensation of the "presence of a love analogous to one that can be read in the smile of a beloved face." However, this was not an experience comparable to that of human love for "we cannot go beyond a certain point in the way of perfection if we think of God only as personal" (*Oeuvres complètes* VI.4.171). In fact, "God is neither personal like us nor impersonal like a thing" (*Oeuvres complètes* VI.2.358).

The rejection of "personalism"[4] plays a role in this conception. "The person within us is our participation in error and sin" (*Ecrits de Londres,* 17; SWR, 318), that part which lays claim to autonomy in its existence. In addition, to go beyond a representation of God as personal, we must on our side render ourselves "similar to an impersonal perfection" (*Oeuvres complètes* VI.4.171; SWR,

318), the form of all perfection—in mathematics as in aesthetic sentiment. In order that God come to us, there must be in our soul "no part that says 'I'" (*Ecrits de Londres,* 17; SWR, 318), as the mystics have understood. Nevertheless, if there is person-to-person contact without the possibility of it being one of our person with a God who is a person "like us," neither can it be the contact of a person with a God who is solely impersonal. Certain passages from her notebooks nevertheless have a curious resonance in this regard: "[God] loves, not as I love, but as an emerald is green" (*Oeuvres complètes* VI.4.171).

Among the reasons to emphasize the impersonal in God are passivity and powerlessness. God is truly all-powerful, but He does not command "everywhere He has the power to do so" (*Oeuvres complètes* IV.1.290). In creating, He delegated His power to necessity, and this is why "in one sense the creature is more powerful than God" (*Oeuvres complètes* VI.4.171). Yet our power is expressed by our capacity to deny, to position ourselves opposite to God, and to hate Him, whereas God loves us unconditionally. Such is His "indifferent power": not able to be other than a gift without reserve. This is what makes God an "impersonal person." Weil adds: "I also, if I were in the state of perfection, would love as an emerald is green. I would be an impersonal person." What, within us, is the very image of God is not "connected with the fact of being a person," but with the "faculty of renouncing personhood" (*Oeuvres complètes* IV.1.313; SWR, 484). We will understand this if we succeed in conceiving God as "impersonal" in a very particular sense: He is "the divine model of a person who goes beyond Himself by renouncing Himself."

This renunciation of power, which, far from turning God into a thing, makes Him a subject, rushes us into a dizzying logic described in the notebooks: we must "love an impersonal God through a personal God (and on the one hand behind a God who is both the one and the other, and on the other hand behind a God who is neither the one nor the other) for fear of falling into conceiving Him as a thing" (*Oeuvres complètes* VI.2.384). God is always subject "so much a subject that even as an object He is still a subject, even as a relationship to an object, He is still a subject" (VI.2.483). This logic, foreign to any dialectic transcendence that would end up in a reconciliation of contradictory elements, reveals the existential mode of the Trinity: "If we think of God solely as one, we would think of Him as being or as act turned toward the outside. To think of Him as act not turned toward the outside, we end up representing Him as two, and at the same time one by the union, that is to say three" (VI.2.460). This union differs from the relationship we know between subject and object, which is abstract; for here this union is a "person."

In revealing her mystical experience to Father Perrin, Weil admitted that she had "halfway refused, not her love, but her intelligence," for one cannot "hold out too long against God if one does so out of pure concern for truth" (*Attente de Dieu,* 45–46; WG, 27). Yet it was not her vocation as a philosopher that kept her from living out a synthesis of intelligence and love for she succeeded in sketching out a harmony between them by defining the domain proper to each one.[5] The torment in Simone Weil was not between philosophy and mysticism. First of all, recall that she experienced within herself a wrenching "in her intelligence and at the center of her heart at the same time" by her inability to "think truthfully at one and the same time about the misery of men, the perfection of God, and the relation between the two" (*Ecrits de Londres,* 213; SL, 178). Later the sudden seizure of divine love did not keep her from experiencing the feeling of her own unworthiness. In the "Prologue" she tells us: "I understood that He[6] had come looking for me by mistake. . . . And yet . . . a point within me could not keep from thinking, as I trembled with fear, that perhaps, in spite of everything, He loves me" (*Oeuvres complètes* VI.3.370). She admitted to Father Perrin that she never reads without trembling the parable of the sterile fig tree in which nature was powerless and that Christ cursed it. She thought that this was a portrait of herself and that this "tore at her heart." It was not that she feared the anger of God, but in a strange reversal, she confessed: "It is the thought of the possible favor of God, of His mercy, which causes me a kind of fear"[7] (*Attente de Dieu,* 84; WG, 52).

In order that the feeling of "misery" that she says does harm to the thoughts within her might disappear, by necessity supernatural love must be everything and she be nothing so that God might be able to love Himself in her. But then she always had the feeling of being "in the way" and of having made "miserably insufficient use" of the "unmerited benefit" she inherited (*Ecrits de Londres,* 209; SL, 175). However losing this insufficiency did not depend on her, for "it is not voluntarily that one can demand" what she dared ask God to grant her in the "decreative" prayer noted down in her notebook: "That I might be without the possibility of bringing about any act of my will, any bodily movement . . . like a complete paralytic. That I might be incapable of receiving any sensation. . . . That I might be without the capacity to put together two thoughts by their slightest relationship, . . . like one of those complete idiots. . . . That I might be insensitive to every kind of sorrow and joy, and incapable of any love for any being" (*Oeuvres complètes* VI.4.279).

The training that led to decreation was directed at the death of the "animals" who in us, with exultation, anguish, or pain, cry out "me, me, me . . . " (*Oeuvres complètes* VI.4.265). This cry has "no meaning and should not be heard by anything or anyone." We can agree with Monique Broc-Lapeyre,[8] however, that "this long apprenticeship of death is a story of love," not to be compared with any natural sentiment. Rather it is a supernatural love by which we give back to God what He has given to us, while denying ourselves any thought of compensation, any temptation to immortality, any idea of a finality, all those consolations that are obstacles to true faith. This is the sense in which Simone Weil saw something purifying in a coherent atheism: "Among those men in whom the supernatural part of themselves has not awakened, the atheists are right and the believers are wrong" (*Oeuvres complètes* VI.2.337). There is a "path toward faith by way of atheism" (*Oeuvres complètes* VI.3.168) that is preferable to a faith that "fills in voids and sweetens bitterness" (*Oeuvres complètes* VI.2.193), a belief which searches "in a dimension in which we cannot make our way" (*Oeuvres complètes* IV.1.278), whereas God alone can cross the distance that separates us from Him.

Should we see all this as "hazardous developments on theological themes,"[9] as Weil suggested in speaking of her notebooks? This would be the case if these developments did not contain coherent elements of a theology of religions, whose inspiration we must at least try to understand.

The Philosophical Cleansing of the Catholic Religion

Simone Weil explicitly rejected syncretism in all areas. In the religious domain, it is necessary "to conceive of the identity of diverse traditions, not by bringing them together according to what they have in common, but by understanding the specific essence that each has. This is a single and same essence" (*Oeuvres complètes* VI.3.202). According to this method, "each religion has its own single truth, that is to say, that when thinking about it, one must give just as much attention to it as if there were no other. . . . A synthesis of religions implies an attention of lesser quality" (*Oeuvres complètes* VI.2.326). Each religion, like every perfectly beautiful work of art, must be approached as an entity perceived in isolation. A hurried comparative approach would mask its spiritual heart. The comparison of religions presupposes a transport "during a certain time, through faith, at the very center of the one that is being studied" (*Oeuvres complètes* IV.1.316; WG, 119). Precisely here there is a question of faith, "in the strongest sense of the word," that is a discernment of the divine within us and around us. This is truly a rare virtue for some have no faith, and others have faith in only one religion, giving to the other religions no more than the attention that might be given to "strangely formed seashells." Still others mistake for impartiality a "vague religiosity which turns indifferently in any direction whatsoever."

Those endowed with authentic discernment ought to use a method of reading that permits them to isolate an ensemble of elements pure enough for them to be found in religions, but equally in folk tales, in legends and mythologies, even in alchemy, heresies, or paganism. This is how she found the Christian dogma of the Trinity in India and among the Greeks. She noticed images of Christ in Greek, Egyptian, Hindu, or Scandinavian mythology, in the Old Testament, in Greek literary figures, or in the principles of geometry.[10] The apprehension of the essence of what is religious goes beyond the notion of a defined truth as something that can be either affirmed or denied. Besides, one would insult "the Catholic faith itself by reducing it to the level of things that can be affirmed or denied" (*Oeuvres complètes* VI.2.343). If Catholicism were true by a truth that makes other religions false, the perception of its truth would block that of the essence of what is religious. Religion "is related to love, not to affirmation or negation." The dogmas of the faith are not things to be affirmed, but "to be contemplated at a certain distance, with attention, respect, and love" (*Lettre à un religieux,* 54; LP, 48). This is all that the Church should be authorized to require, excluding any commandment to adhere to its dogmas.

This makes it possible to understand the position of Simone Weil with regard to Catholicism and the Church. She insisted to Father Perrin that Christianity should "contain within itself all vocations without exception, since it is catholic." It is "catholic by entitlement but not in fact" (*Attente de Dieu,* 52; WG, 32). In context, this formula signifies that the vocation of Christianity is to make Christ incarnate in each people and its culture, but in no way with the purpose of substituting itself for their traditions. This conception leads to a logic of the inclusion of traditions.[11] Clearly there must be opposition to a logic of exclusion characteristic of the historical practice of anathema or of the Inquisition, but equally there is the question of escaping from an imperialist conception of inclusion whose aim would be to absorb other traditions. There must be neither obliteration nor exclusion, but rather an unveiling of the implicit in other traditions while preserving in them their singularity and their context. In this sense, one cannot say that "what is not Christian is false, but: all that is true is Christian" (*Oeuvres complètes* VI.3.395).

This does not mean that Christianity fulfills the truth to which other religions give only imperfect witness. Weil rejects the normative version of Christianity according to which whatever is true and good in other religions exists only in a degraded form or in the form of a distant preparation that Christianity would complete. It is precisely in their otherness that the elements of truth and goodness, which structure the other religions, must be recognized. She proposed to lay out what should be the future of a *de facto* Catholicism by listing all that she loves and does not wish to abandon, but which have remained outside Christianity: "all the vast panorama of centuries past, except for the last twenty; all the lands inhabited by races of color; the whole of secular life in countries of the white race; in the history of these countries, all the traditions accused of heresy, like the Manichean and Albigensian tradition; all those things issued from the Renaissance, too often degraded, but not completely without value" (*Attente de Dieu*, 52–53; WG, 32).

The Catholic Church is perceived as a "society of the sacred" which has lost its capacity to reveal all that is pure in the other traditions. This incapacity—outside the power inherited from Rome—values its heritage from the Hebrew religion. There is a price to pay for the monotheism of the Old Testament, that of exclusion by the radical distinction between truth and error. This exclusion prevents any agreement between different religions, whose essence would otherwise be identical. The exclusivism of the God of Israel would prevent a reading of other religions, affirming itself as Truth in opposition to idolatry. On the contrary, Catholicism should fulfill its true universal nature looking back (toward its past traditions) and forward beyond itself (the rise of new images of Christianity).

The insistence that her own thought be both indifferent and welcoming to "all ideas without exception" defined for Weil a vocation which required her "to remain outside the Church, without even an implicit commitment to the Church or to Christian dogma" (*Attente de Dieu*, 65; WG, 40). She knew that here there was a question of a "position of unstable equilibrium," but she hoped that her "fidelity," for which God would not refuse her the grace, would permit her to "remain there indefinitely without budging, *en hupomone*"[12] (*Attente de Dieu*, 66; WG, 41). The expression "unstable equilibrium" attenuates the paradox she revealed in a confidential statement she made to several correspondents. For example she wrote to Thibon: "I have the impression that I am lying whatever I may do, whether by remaining outside the Church, or by entering if I should do so. The question is to know which is the lesser lie."[13] The "lesser lie" in this situation is also for her a form of fidelity to "the aspect of truth" that she perceives and that she would betray if she left that point of the "intersection of Christianity and all that it is not " (*Attente de Dieu*, 54; WG, 32).

One of the consequences of this attitude is that this revelation is not considered as a unique act, which would oppose Christianity to other religions. Cardinal Danielou objected that conversion to Christianity is the passage from religion to revelation. Yet he expressed perfectly Weil's position when he wrote that "much more than her being led to accept the newness of Christianity, [she] would be tempted to love in it the persistence of an original truth."[14] According to her, in fact, revelation is universal and permanent. Just as the ways to salvation impregnate religious traditions other than Christianity, revelation sows in them and in diverse cultures true and pure elements of the divine mystery. Even the hypothesis of a destruction of the "temporal existence of Christianity" did not

keep Weil from imagining the "possibility, after several genera-
tions, of a new revelation" (*Oeuvres complètes* VI.2.476).

This position does not mean the negation of Christ's Incarnation. The search for traces of revelation in all religions is carried
out by the mediation of Christ, "his redemptive suffering carrying
the presence of God to the ends of the earth by the cooperation
of the creature." God made himself a creature "so that one day for
sure this work would be accomplished perfectly. The Cross is the
very essence of the Incarnation" (*Oeuvres complètes* VI.2.469–70).
If Christ is the incomparable mediator, it is because He is the very
event of the Incarnation of God all the way to total degradation:
Christ died as one condemned by common law, not as a martyr.[15]
Here we find the central motive of Weil's spirituality, the privilege of the path of suffering, which is "in one sense the very essence of creation"[16] (*Oeuvres complètes* IV.1.369; SWS, 66). This
path was the path of Christ, and as such is the interpretive model
of the Cross: the Cross—not the Glory or the resurrection—"the
only source of radiance luminous enough to shed light on suffering" to the point that "at any epoch or in any country whatsoever,
wherever there is some form of suffering, the Cross of Christ is
its truth."[17] On the presupposition that suffering is the essence of
Creation, the pre-eminence of the Cross is based as a nonexclusive
model of multiple incarnations in other traditions.

Gradually, Weil put into place the elements of a "philosophical cleansing of the Catholic religion" (*Oeuvres complètes* VI.2.438)
needed due to difficulties "of a philosophical order" concerning the
"precisions with which the Church felt the necessity of surround-
ing [its mysteries] throughout the centuries" (*Ecrits de Londres*,
198; SL, 155). Certainly, the intelligence cannot control mystery
itself, "but [the intelligence] is in perfect possession of the power of
control over the paths that lead to mystery, that rise to it, and the
paths that lead down again" (*Oeuvres complètes* VI.4.174). With
respect to the Church, this means that in it the presence of Christ
in the Eucharist alone is unconditioned. On the other hand, the

Church, as "a society issuing opinions, is a phenomenon of this world—conditioned."

These "opinions" require a cleansing by the intelligence. In fact, in order to be transported above the domain of the intelligence, one must have made beforehand "the most logical, the most rigorous use" of intelligence, to the very limit of its possibilities, "otherwise one is not above, but below." Even if, from the point of view of the intelligence, contact with the transcendent—the "real reality" (*Oeuvres complètes* VI.2.438)—appears contradictory, it is certain that, once supernatural love has been experienced, this contact is real, for "our faculties are incapable of making [this] up" (VI 2.343). The soul in which supernatural love exists must, by means of its intelligence, know that what is not apprehended by the intelligence "is more real than what is apprehended." This implies that the intelligence, the faculty "most precious after love" (*Lettre à un religieux,* 66; LP, 58), possesses "in its own nature a constraining motive sufficient to subordinate itself to supernatural love" (*Oeuvres complètes* VI.4.174). To this end, the soul must enjoy "total liberty in its own domain" (*Lettre à un religieux,* 69; LP, 62). If faith has the possibility of becoming "the experience of the intelligence being enlightened by love" (*Oeuvres complètes* VI.2.340), then supernatural love, far from crushing reason and intelligence, must be its generator.

Anti-Hebraism, Anti-Judaism, or Anti-Semitism?

In Christianity, "almost from its origin," there is a "malaise of the intelligence" (*Attente de Dieu,* 57; WG, 34). How far back must we go to find this "origin"? One element of the answer is in a passage that sets the tone for what Father Perrin called her "horror for Israel":[18] "Everything in Christianity that is inspired by the Old Testament is bad, beginning with the conception of the sanctity of the Church, modeled on that of the sanctity of Israel" (*Pensées sans ordre,* 52). Even when she appears positive, regarding certain biblical persons or regarding certain books she admired more than others, it is only to reproach Israel once again for what she judges "assimilable for a Christian soul" (*Lettre à un religieux,* 71; LP, 64). She considers that "until the exile, there is not a single person of the Hebrew race mentioned in the Bible whose life is not defiled by horrible things," except Daniel, but he had been "initiated into Chaldean wisdom" (*Pensées sans ordre,* 57). Job, another example, "was a Mesopotamian, not a Jew" (*Oeuvres complètes* IV.1.381). This method of interpretation led her to see in the first part of Genesis "a transposition of Egyptian accounts more or less well understood and adapted" (*Oeuvres complètes* VI.4.287). Those passages from the Old Testament acceptable to a Christian should then be uprooted from the Jewish tradition.[19]

All the complaints of Simone Weil can be attributed to her interpretation of the concept of God in the Old Testament. She admitted that she could not understand "how it is possible for a reasonable mind to regard the Jehovah of the Bible and the Father invoked in the Gospel as one and the same being" (*Pensées sans ordre,* 64; SL, 129–30). The mission of Israel was to recognize the unicity of God, but that unicity remained inseparable from a moral blindness of the Hebrews, who believed in "one God without distinction of persons or of principles of good and evil" (*Oeuvres complètes* VI.3.296). The Hebrews attributed to God all that is supernatural, what is divine as well as what is demonic, a confusion which derives from their conception of God "under the attribute of power and not under the attribute of Good" (*Pensées sans ordre,* 55). If there is an absolute principle for Simone Weil, it is that the "essential knowledge concerning God is that God is the Good" (*Pensées sans ordre,* 47). The Egyptians had this knowledge, the Greeks had it, but not the Hebrews. The God of the Hebrews was a "carnal and collective" God, an "oppressive" God, who made temporal promises. By rejecting a "national god" Weil refused the notion of a chosen people, "incompatible with the knowledge of the true God," for this is the worst of idolatries (*Pensées sans ordre*, 51). A conception of God under the attribute of power alone leads us to conceive of Him without an intermediary. Now, "there can be no person to person contact between man and God except through the person of a Mediator" (*Oeuvres complètes* VI.3.297). Without a Mediator, which means that "no one goes to God, creator and sovereign, without passing through God EMPTIED OF HIS DIVINITY" (*Oeuvres complètes* VI.2.393), God becomes a directly accessible reality, racial, social, or national.[20]

Weil did not know very much about Judaism, but this is not what is essential. What do we learn from essays like "Les trois fils de Noé et l'histoire de la civilisation méditerranéenne," "Note sur les relations primitives du christianisme et des religions non hébraïques," or "Israël et les 'Gentils'"?[21] Their reading reveals a distortion in Weil's method. In a letter to Father Perrin, she conceded that passages from the Gospels that used to shock her had become "extremely illuminating," and that, if she had not "read and re-read them with love, [she] would not have been able to arrive at the truth" she found in them (*Attente de Dieu,* 249). She insisted that she had the "same attitude of mind with regard to other religious or metaphysical traditions and other sacred texts." This means that she read the mythologies, Pythagoras, Plato and the Greek stoics, universal folklore, the *Upanishads* and the *Bhagavad-Gita,* the Chinese Taoist writings, those of the Zen Buddhist movement, the sacred Egyptian texts, and even certain heresies,[22] all in the same mental attitude as when she read the Gospels. She did not read the Old Testament in this same state of mind. In the face of different religious and metaphysical traditions, the intelligence ought to be capable of receiving the light of love, the experience that defines faith. But, when there is a question of the Old Testament, love, the "organ in us through which we see God" (*Oeuvres complètes* VI.2.340), does not find a way to invest in the God of the Hebrews. Everything happened then as if the conditions of a good orientation of attention were lacking, as if the "duty of intellectual probity" that Weil considered inseparable from her vocation had faded away. In her relation to the Old Testament and Jewishness, what was this risk to her intelligence and love that made her unable to bring her project into conformity with her vocation? To speak of "self-hatred" or of anti-Semitism[23] when she encounters the "Jewish Question" does not lead to an understanding of this hardening of an intellectual and spiritual orientation that elsewhere lacks neither intelligence nor love.

On the Threshold of the Church

Simone Weil's "spiritual progression"[24] was structured by other refusals and other reservations, not all of them overcome, as was the case with prayer and the sacraments of Baptism and the Eucharist. Her "spiritual autobiography" reveals that she prayed "in the literal sense of the word" beginning in September 1941 as she worked harvesting grapes at Saint-Julien-de-Peyrolas. During that summer she had repeated the Our Father word for word in Greek with Thibon and had set herself to reciting it each day before and during her work in the vineyards. This practice deepened over time and led to her mystical experience.

Another factor in her spiritual progress was her adherence to the mystery of the Eucharist during the winter of 1941–42. She felt intensely what she called her "hunger" for the Eucharist during her stay at the Abbaye de Solesmes, where a young English retreatant gave her "for the first time the idea of the supernatural power of the sacraments" by the radiance that "seemed to clothe him after he received communion" (*Attente de Dieu*, 43; WG, 26). The "Prologue" evokes the presence in an attic of a mysterious visitor who brought from a cupboard a loaf that "had the true taste of bread" and wine that "had the taste of the sun and the earth" (*Oeuvres complètes* VI.3.369), an evident reference to the eucharistic meal. In Marseille, Weil went to the convent of the Dominican nuns to spend some moments in silence in the Cenacle chapel of the religious where the Blessed Sacrament was exposed.[25] Faithful to her position "on the threshold of the Church," she nevertheless wrote to Father Perrin: "Only now my heart has been transported, forever, I hope, into the Blessed Sacrament exposed on the altar" (*Attente de Dieu,* 54; WG, 32).

She herself established the relationship between the two new elements of her spirituality when, after having recalled the sense of deliverance brought about by the recitation of the Our Father, she confided that it was exactly the same "if one looks at the Blessed Sacrament without any thought other than that Christ is there" (*Oeuvres complètes* IV.1.282). "If one looks . . ." she insisted. She wrote to Maritain in July 1942: "I remain on the threshold of the Church, my eyes fixed on the Blessed Sacrament, but without daring to take a step. When I see people receiving communion, I truly experience hunger; till now I have never had the feeling that God wants me to appease this hunger by entering into the Church"[26] (*Cahiers Simone Weil* [June 1980]: 70). In addition, in a letter to Schumann, recalling the words of Christ according to which "the Son of Man must be lifted up like the serpent of Moses, so that those who believe in Him might be saved," she commented, "I think that, with this in mind, looking at the host and chalice during the elevation constitutes a sacrament" (*Ecrits de Londres,* 205; SL, 172).

When she came to the problem of baptism as she saw it, Weil affirmed that, in her case, "to be born by Water and the Spirit, [she] had to abstain from visible water" (*Attente de Dieu,* 65; WG, 40). The difficulty she experienced in discussing the question with Father Perrin led her to consult Canon Vidal, superior of the major seminary of Carcassonne. In this interview[27] she saw herself as justified by his recognition in her of an "(implicit) desire for baptism," but the canon expressed a doctrinal position by adding that she would not hesitate to receive it "if she had the necessary lights," those afforded by the Church. Back in Marseille, she confided to a friend: "As our conversations continued, I saw baptism retreating farther and farther away from me." The acceptance of a "baptism of desire" was not sufficient for her. She wanted to know if, by not renouncing any of the implications of her particular vocation, she would be able to receive a sacrament that would open to her the gates of the real Church, "in an overpowering manner, and not by the isolated initiative of a priest performing an obscure and unknown baptism" (*Pensées sans ordre*, 152). Her baptism by an understanding and generous priest would not be enough to make manifest that urgent and vital breaking off of the Church from a "routine of at least seventeen centuries" (*Pensées sans ordre*, 151), which she demanded without fail.

In 1942 she expressed "what she had been thinking for years," namely that the bonds that attached her to the Catholic faith were becoming "more and more profoundly rooted in her heart and her intelligence," while at the same time, the thoughts that distanced her from the Church were "also growing in force and clarity" (*Lettre à un religieux*, 13–14; LP, 9). Simultaneously, in a wrenching she never overcame, she distanced herself further and further from her demand for baptism, and she lived intensely her desire for the sacraments of which the Church was the depositary. At the beginning of her stay in Marseille, Weil felt "as close as possible to Catholicism yet without being Catholic." Toward the end of her stay, she confided to Simone Pétrement: "I did not believe I was closer to Catholicism and yet I had approached much nearer" (*La Vie*, 532; SWL, 394). "Approached," this did not prevent her, at the very same moment, from declaring firmly that she felt "in a definitive and certain way" that her vocation required her to have no kind of commitment to the Church. She interpreted her particular vocation as an obligation to remain on the threshold, while waiting for Christianity to become *de facto* Catholic.[28]

chapter five

Decreation,

Completing Creation

"God abdicated in giving us existence," wrote Simone Weil in her notebook (*Oeuvres complètes* VI.4.347). Because He gave up exercising power in this world by decreation, He can be present in Creation "only under a form of absence" (VI.3.105). He withdrew so that we might be. How do we rejoin Him or more exactly how do we bring about the possibility that He lead us back to Himself?[1]

By abdicating, God accomplishes a twofold movement: He "makes Himself necessity"[2] (VI.2.266), and He offers us free existence. In this world there can be no harmony between pure necessity and pure freedom. We must consent to their separation and make use of it as a lever to raise ourselves to the supernatural. We can make supernatural use of a necessity we cannot control, whether it be our inescapable servitude in work, the affliction that is the result of our condition, or the sorrow and the suffering that our intelligence does not understand. It is the whole experience of decreation that in the annihilation of the self constitutes a perfect imitation of Christ.[3]

The necessity that rules our world is in essential continuity with God. Matter, completely subject to necessity, is a model of obedience to God; it is a mirror of supernatural reality. Properly speaking, there is Creation to the extent that the existence given us introduces an obstacle between God and God. Weil compared human existence, placed under the sign of appearance and illusion, to "non-being that looks like being" (VI.4.124). The "impression of being someone" destroys the harmony of the good (God) and of necessity (matter) by creating in man the vague desire to transform the human condition by persuading him that his freedom is capable of anything. If between God and us there is "something like equality," it is solely in the absolute freedom we have to "consent or not to the orientation toward Him that He has imprinted in us" (IV.1.336; SWR, 490).

So we have the choice between two forms of obedience to necessity, obedience without consent or obedience with consent. It is up to us to distinguish the two forms carefully. We owe nothing to false necessity for this is an effect of the oppression against which we have the obligation to struggle. On the other hand, faced with the necessity that comes from the order of things, freedom has been given us so that we may be able to make the choice of renouncing it. To consent to the order of things is to obey necessity and beyond that the will of God who wished that it be thus. From this logic, Weil drew a radical consequence, pushing to its paroxysm of rigor the motive of the annihilation of self, which is at the heart of her mystical experience: "God can love in us only this consent to step back and let Him pass" (*Oeuvres complètes* VI.3.86) as a response to that step back by which He Himself let us be.

The Path of Affliction

There is the alleged "masochism" of Weil. Nevertheless, she states clearly that she believes in the "value of suffering as long as everything possible is done to avoid it [which is honest]"[4] (*Oeuvres complètes* VI.1.139). She also wrote that "the suffering we inflict upon ourselves, however intense, however long, however violent it may be, is not destructive." This particular suffering is not the "true response to the excess of divine love." The true response "consists solely in consenting to the possibility of being destroyed . . . whether that suffering is realized or not" (*Intuitions pre-chrétiennes*, 148; IC, 183). Actually, affliction is a "pulverizing of the soul by the mechanical brutality of circumstances"; it is what "is imposed on man against his will"[5] (*Oeuvres complètes* IV.1.369; SWS, 65). Man must force himself "to avoid affliction, solely in order that the affliction encountered might prove perfectly pure and perfectly bitter" (*Oeuvres complètes* VI.2.417). This is a condition for a proper "use of the supernatural," completely foreign to the "search for a supernatural remedy against suffering" (*Oeuvres complètes* VI.3.64).

Our exposure to affliction entails different degrees. Our flesh is exposed to the brutality of matter and our soul is "pitifully dependent on all manner of things and beings that are in themselves fragile and capricious." Our social person, which is so dependent on "the sense of our existence," is "exposed to all manner of unexpected occurrences." Let us emphasize this last point for "there is no true affliction where there is not some form or other of degradation or the apprehension of such degradation" (*Oeuvres complètes* IV.1.348; SWS, 43). Affliction must not be confounded with one of its degrees; it implies simultaneously the three experiences of brutal violence, of hopeless distress, and of humiliating social degradation. These conditions were perfectly realized by Christ. This is why Weil separated Christ from the martyrs persecuted for their faith for they were not afflicted: "Christ was afflicted" because he died as a "common criminal, mixed in with thieves, only somewhat more subject to ridicule" (*Oeuvres complètes* IV.1.352; SWS, 47). Christ's abandonment was expressed in his cry that broke the silence: "The principal effect of affliction is to force the soul to cry out 'why', as Christ Himself did, and to repeat this cry uninterruptedly. . . . If [the soul] does not renounce love, it ends up one day hearing . . . the silence as something even infinitely more significant than any response, like the very word of God. . . . The cry of Christ and the silence of the Father together create a supreme harmony" (*Intuitions pre-chrétiennes,* 167–69; IC, 198–99).

What must be noted here is the coherence of this "path of affliction" with the conception of God the Creator who, by creating, annihilates Himself, going to the very limit of Himself. This Christology would lead Weil to limit herself to the evidence of Good Friday rather than go on to the "rejoicing of Easter Sunday."[6] She told Father Couturier: "If the Gospel made no mention of the Resurrection of Christ, faith would be easier for me," even adding that the Cross has on her "the same effect that the Resurrection has on others" (*Lettre à un religieux,* 62–63). She states in opposition to St. Paul that "the agony on the Cross is something more divine than the Resurrection" (*Intuitions pre-chrétiennes,* 84; IC, 143). So she was consistent with herself when she declared with irrepressible certitude that God could not be encountered in His truth until she found herself "in one of these present extreme forms of affliction" (*Ecrits de Londres,* 213; SL, 178).

Corresponding to this idea that the Incarnation culminates in the death on the Cross and not in the Resurrection, there are other passages in which Weil seems to challenge the belief in the immortality of the soul as "harmful" inasmuch as "belief in the prolonging of life eliminates the use of death" (*Oeuvres complètes* VI.3.192). The "use of death" is our consent at this moment of truth that "teaches us that we do not exist except as one thing among many others" (*Oeuvres complètes* VI.4.334). By consenting to our weakness all the way to annihilation, void of any meaning or finality, we penetrate the realm of truth.[7]

Other Paths to Decreation

Attention must be exercised in a void, in that operation by which we turn ourselves toward an object while detaching the spirit from particular ends pursued by the self. This requirement does not keep Weil from describing attention as a desire. It is often thought that desire drives the energy of the self to seek its own expansion. Yet, as she wrote, "Desire truly exists when there is an effort at attention" (*Oeuvres complètes* IV.1.257; SWS, 93), a purified desire that has eliminated every motive other than the good and the truth. Attention gives back to the real what the existence of the self has stolen from it. The self, conscious of danger, feels repugnance "for true attention much more violently than the flesh finds fatigue repugnant," and this repugnance is "closer to evil than is the flesh." In addition, each moment of attention "destroys some evil within us" (*Oeuvres complètes* IV.1.259; SWS, 96). This is the formative role of scholastic exercises that, even if they develop only the attention that reasons, are able to "prepare for the appearance in the soul of its highest form, intuitive attention," an attention which "turned directly toward God, constitutes true prayer"[8] (*La Condition ouvrière*, 430). Attention is decreative. "Like the desire to become more apt at grasping the truth" (*Oeuvres complètes* IV.1.257; SWS, 93), attention prepares the soul to receive the light that descends from above. Yet it is not the only thing that is capable of contributing to this preparation.

"To hear the divine silence," Weil writes, "one must have been constrained to seek in vain some finality here below. Only two things have the power to impose this constraint: either affliction, or the pure joy that results from the feeling of beauty" (*Intuitions pre-chrétiennes*, 168; IC, 199). "Pure joy" is a joy that has nothing to do with an expansion of our personal existence. As a matter of fact, "perfect joy excludes the very feeling of joy, for in the soul filled by the object, no corner is available to say 'I'" (*Oeuvres complètes* VI.2.251). Such a joy, from which every association with the self is removed, is a sentiment of the real, not of the self. In this way I experience the joy that there is sunshine or that the moon is shining over the sea; the self formulates no demands with regard to these realities. There is "no *I* in the plenitude of joy" (*Oeuvres complètes* VI.2.403), only a sentiment of the real, which is decreative.

Beauty, thanks to this power to snatch us from any particular inclination of the self, is defined as "God's trap" (*Oeuvres complètes* VI.4.373) to conquer the soul. Weil interprets the Kantian theory according to which beauty, "without containing any particular finality, . . . gives the imperious feeling of the presence of a finality" (*Intuitions pré-chrétiennes,* 168; IC, 199). The disinterested aesthetic sentiment gently inclines us toward the form of a non-representable end, of a presence that is a supreme absence. Consequently, like affliction, beauty confronts something "impenetrable to the intelligence" (*Oeuvres complètes* VI.2.432). Playing a role in multiple plans permits beauty to run through those plans as well as go beyond them; beauty is the only being of the intelligible world that appears to the senses: beauty testifies to the perceived order of the universe, of the equilibrium of the necessary relations that the intelligence can grasp. In beauty, necessity becomes an object of love.

One might think that Weil's spiritual itinerary had been completed by decreation. This, however, would be to overlook the other side of her spirituality, that of a platonism suited to the conditions of our existence. To approach this side, we return to the consequence of her crossing a spiritual threshold regarding work. Other human activities are "inferior in spiritual signification to physical work" (*L'Enracinement,* 380; NR, 302) for consent to necessity in work offers to the greatest number the possibility of perceiving necessity "under the aspect of obedience," and "this knowledge is supernatural" (*Oeuvres complètes* VI.3.405, 407). The experience of work in time, lived out as a form of servitude, is equally its spiritual strength, creating from one instant to another the experience of an obedience analogous to that of inert matter that "continues through one instant after another" (*L'Enracinement,* 379; NR, 301).

In order to have a clear understanding of Weil's position, we must insist on the fact that, in spite of the value of a work that would imitate an abandonment to the time of things, in her eyes it remained true that "there is a certain relation with time that is suited to inert things, and another that is suited to thinking creatures. It would be wrong to confuse them" (*L'Enracinement,* 83; NR, 60). Consequently, no praise for an annihilation that would be a degradation. Acceptance or consent is suitable for "inevitable physical and moral sufferings to the precise degree that they are inevitable" (*La Condition ouvrière,* 232). Conscious consent to inevitable necessity has nothing to do with the docility produced by a "taming which calls for nothing that is properly human" (*La Condition ouvrière,* 323–24). We must not misinterpret the "penal" character of work, which is a penalty, but which "in itself is not a degradation" (*Ecrits de Londres,* 22; SWR, 322). Work is penal, not like a punishment inflicted by a will that decrees, but like a reminder of obedience to natural necessity that defines our condition. God is simply reminding us of the order of the world He has created by burying His power in necessity. Consequently, there is no contradiction between the "the old law": "You will earn your bread by the sweat of your brow (curse)" and "the new law: Control nature by obeying it" (*Oeuvres complètes* VI.1.92). The "curse of work" consists in this, that whoever seeks to control nature in this world, distinct from the terrestrial Paradise, must obey its inexorable necessities. "Disenchantment with the world" constitutes the first meaning of the original malediction, but modernity misinterprets this disenchantment by forgetting obedience, believing that this disenchanted world is subject to our exaggerated power. On the contrary, work should enter into a balanced *reading* of the world as a "text with several significations" the entire breadth of which must be perceived on several levels: those of the flesh, of the intelligence, of attention, of obedience, of intuition, and of beauty.[9] A reading done in this way would renew the "pact of the spirit with the universe."[10]

Signifying the Absolute in This World

Like Plato, Simone Weil refused to block the path of the wise man as he was leaving the cave to contemplate the Good. Certainly the soul must turn its back completely on that "perpetual mixture of becoming and annihilation" (*La Source grecque,* 86; SNL, 104), which the world is, to turn itself toward the Real. However, the simple uprooting of any concerns about the world cannot bring about the salvation of the philosopher or the saint. Recalling what she called "authentic elites," recognizable by their spiritual discernment, Weil warned that it was not a question of founding a "new Franciscan order" living in a convent in rough brown habits. On the contrary, "these people must be in the masses and touch them without anything coming in between" (*Ecrits de Londres,* 105; SE, 216). The notebooks describe "an order of religious without habit or emblem, who would be imbued with the highest aesthetic, philosophic, and theological culture, and who would then go down through the years abstaining from any religious practice unless the circumstances required it like criminals in the prisons, like workers in factories, like peasants in the fields" (*Oeuvres complètes* VI.3.65–66). In other words, in order to go to the real and to God, the wise man or the saint should cast on this terrestrial life "the reflection of supernatural light" in order to turn this life and this world into a reality, "for up to this point they are no more than dreams. It is incumbent on him to achieve creation in this way" (*La Source grecque,* 96; SNL, 112).

Nothing better sums up her refusal of a spirituality that would oppose this unreal world to the intelligible (or supernatural) world than this affirmation: "The object of my research is not the supernatural, but this world. The supernatural is the light. We must not dare to make of it an object. Otherwise we debase it"[11] (*Oeuvres complètes* VI.2.245). Weil conceives of work, technique, and science as procedures of purification that lead the soul "to feel almost at home in the place of its exile" (*Sur la science,* 235) in such a way that the order of the universe becomes an object of love. To this end we should find a science[12] and forms of technology that imply a rupture of our perspective of limitless domination over the world. Technology, work, and science could then contribute, along with art, to impregnating the world with a reality whose order could reveal God, its author, as a "real metaphor" (*Oeuvres complètes* VI.4.114), manifesting for us "the supreme poet" (101).

The care of the soul passes through concerns about the conditions to be realized here below, at the heart of our civilization considered in what is most characteristic of it: "Everyone repeats . . . that we are suffering from an imbalance due to a purely material development of technology. This imbalance can be adjusted only by a spiritual development in the same domain, that is to say, in the domain of work" (*L'Enracinement,* 128; NR, 98). From this point of view, meditation on social phenomena is a "purification of the first importance," and Weil considered that she "was not wrong to be involved in politics over so many years," for "*contemplating* the social is just as good a path as retiring from the world" (*Oeuvres complètes* VI.2.434–35). By completing creation in this way we will arrive at the best *reading*: that of necessity behind the sensible, of order behind necessity, then of God behind that order. No stage, no domain can be neglected, for the "rigorously scientific [study] of supernatural mechanisms" must not forget that the good comes down from heaven "only in proportion as certain conditions are actually realized here on earth" (*L'Enracinement,* 332–33; NR, 264).

It is idolatry to consider that "here below one or several objects enclose [the] absolute." In any case, only through such objects "can human love penetrate to what exists behind them" (*L'Enracinement,* 201; NR, 158). This is the problem of *L'Enracinement*. There must be institutions that make the signification of the absolute possible in this world. Certainly, institutions that protect rights, persons, and freedoms already exist, but "beyond them . . . others must be found destined to abolish, in contemporary life, anything that crushes souls under injustice, the lie, and ugliness" (*Ecrits de Londres,* 44; SWR, 339). Weil wrote "beyond" and not "in their place." A foundation must be provided for the "middle region of values" (*Ecrits de Londres,* 29; SWR, 328), but the institutions that protect law, persons, and liberties "can be put to good use in their region" (*Ecrits de Londres,* 43; SWR, 338). These are surprising statements for us, who tend to see a recourse against totalitarianism in the elevation of these values to the summit of the legal edifice. The difficulty is to guard against a hasty reading of *L'Enracinement* that would conclude that a spiritual impregnation would be sufficient to take the place of institutions and solutions to political and social problems. Once again, this would be a case of forgetting the key expression: the distinction of levels.

How is the principle of the arrangement of values in the "middle region" to be determined according to the demands of a superior domain? First of all, it has to be understood that the "bond which attaches the human being to the other reality is, like that other reality, beyond the reach of all human faculties," but it must be understood as well that for that bond there is "the possibility of an indirect expression." This leads to the recognition that the "respect inspired by man's bond with the reality outside this world is a testimony of that part of man which is situated in the reality of this world" (*Ecrits de Londres,* 77; SWA, 77). Such are the givens of the problem.

The very first sentence of *L'Enracinement* defines what provides an orientation toward a "reality foreign to this world." It is *obligation,* a notion that "takes precedence over that of rights, which is subordinate and relative to it." In fact, I am unconditionally obligated, to myself and to anyone else, even to someone who claims no rights for himself (or who would not feel himself obligated to me); as for the person who insists on a right, this right does not become effective for him unless someone else considers himself obligated toward him. Consequently, each right is relative to an obligation toward others that someone accepts for himself; every claim to a right for myself is relative to the recognition of my own obligations and to the recognition by others of their obligations. Whether of right or of obligation, only the second notion can be considered an absolute. Weil can then show that rights, considered in isolation, are linked to notions "of sharing, of exchange, of quantity" and that there is "something commercial about it" (*Ecrits de Londres*, 23; SWR, 323). Being "a bit above brutal force," it needs force "to confirm it, otherwise it is ridiculous." Always, when taken in isolation, a right is efficacious only if a balance of forces has already been established. So this is not a question of challenging the Rights of Man; they must be given a coherence that the men of 1789 could not give them. They "began with the notion of right" and "at the same time, they wanted to establish absolute principles," which is a conceptually contradictory process, a "confusion of language and ideas, which plays an important role in our present political and social confusion" (*L'Enracinement*, 10; NR, 4).

If the notion of "person" finds a place in the "middle region," it is because the notion of right has dragged it there, "for right is related to personal things" (*Ecrits de Londres*, 27; SWR, 326). On this subject, nothing can replace the reading of her essay dedicated to "La Personne et le Sacré" ("Human Personality") in the *Ecrits de Londres*. Let us recall the essential, namely that what is sacred in man is what "uproots [him] from the particularity of the self" (*Ecrits de Londres*, 17; SWR, 318). The person, under the form of those talents that distinguish it socially, is so closely bound to the collectivity that it is what can be entirely broken in us under the effect of a daily constraint, which is exactly what Weil experienced in the factory. Her conclusion is peremptory: "It is impossible to define respect for the human person. . . . To take as a rule for public morality a notion that is impossible to define or even conceive is to open the door to every kind of tyranny" (*Ecrits de Londres*,

12; SWR, 314). To speak of the "rights of the human person" is to mix together "two insufficient notions." It becomes necessary and justified to replace the pair *right/person* by the pair *obligation/needs of the soul.*

This introduction to the notion of vital need will orient us toward the solution of the problem as posed: how to attribute to that "part of man situated in the reality of this world" the respect inspired by what attaches him to the absolute outside this world? The possibility of an "indirect expression" of respect for human beings establishes an obligation, which has as its object the "terrestrial needs of the soul and of the body." "To each need there is a corresponding obligation. To each obligation there is a corresponding need" (*Ecrits de Londres*, 78; SWS, 136), and this is why obligation permits us to run the entire gamut from the most elevated "principle" to the most "concrete detail" (*Ecrits de Londres*, 170), which are the needs of the soul and those of the body here below.

This principle leads us to the "ability to pass over to the impersonal" (*Ecrits de Londres*, 155). What makes it possible for us to enter into contact with the impersonal part of the soul is the cry of the afflicted person: "Why are they doing me harm?"—a cry that expresses the demand for justice and creates an obligation for us. Such a cry signifies an "impersonal protestation" (*Ecrits de Londres*, 16; SWR, 317) in the sense that it expresses that "something" in every man who "invincibly expects that good be done to him and not evil" (*Ecrits de Londres*, 13; SWR, 315); it wells up in the center of the heart, from a "demand for an absolute good that always dwells there" (*Ecrits de Londres*, 74; SWA, 202). Right cannot define the respect for that part of the soul because "the revolt of the entire being" (*Ecrits de Londres*, 22; SWR, 322) against the evil that is being done to him has nothing to do with the claim for a right, a claim that always implies something of an exchange. "[T]he revolt of the entire being" expresses something in each individual that can be neither exchanged, nor paid for, nor compensated since in this case it is a demand for an absolute good.

This can be understood more easily by referring to an example. Simone Weil reminds us that for those whose work is debased by oppression no compensation is possible by raises in salary because there is no price for the purchase of a soul. One must not sell his debasement at the highest price nor be resigned to an evil done to him by men. On the basis of the refusal of quantitative compensations for servitude, the resistance of workers "would have an impulse entirely different from what the thought of their persons and their rights could furnish them" (*Ecrits de Londres,* 22; SWR, 322). It is a question of furnishing an energy superior to resistance against oppression, by opposing to it the obligation to respect the satisfaction of a vital need: the equal possibility, offered to all by work, to have access to an "impersonal form of attention."

The "needs of the soul" and the needs of the body are strongly bound together to the point that the "list of obligations toward the human being must correspond to the list of those human needs that are vital, analogous to hunger" (*L'Enracinement,* 13–14; NR, 6). This model makes possible a record of these needs, the forms of which may vary, but their essence is universal. *L'Enracinement* lays out fifteen needs of the soul, to which must be added "establishing roots," introduced at the beginning of the second part of the book, but which is the "most important and the most misunderstood need of the human soul" (61; NR, 43). Most needs of the soul are "arranged in opposed pairs that balance and complete one another" (*Ecrits de Londres,* 81; SWA, 208): freedom and obedience, responsibility and initiative, equality and hierarchy, honor and punishment, freedom of opinion and truth, security and risk, private property and public property. Order, the first need considered, does not enter into any of the opposed pairs—no more so than rootedness (*enracinement*)—for it is "over and above needs, properly so-called" (*L'Enracinement,* 20; NR, 11–12).

Why treat the other needs of the soul in opposed pairs? Already in 1937, Weil noticed that throughout history men often fought "over words empty of any meaning" (*Oeuvres complètes* II.3.51;

SWR, 168), such as nation, security, capitalism, or communism. One of the characteristics of these words is to live in antagonistic pairs, each appearing, according to the situation, as the absolute incarnation of freedom, democracy, justice, dictatorship, or absolute evil. Each term is handled as if it intrinsically contained its own particular virtue or evil. All reality is defined by relations and conditions of existence. The good use of words is not to isolate them, but to place the notions that they express in *real* oppositions. This avoids debasing them into slogans.

As an example let us take the word 'order'. It draws the imagination toward an immediate adhesion or repulsion. But Weil does not oppose order to disorder; she does not introduce the notion into a pair of opposites, and yet order is not considered an absolute, for to think of it "there must be a knowledge of other needs" (*L'Enracinement,* 20; NR, 12), of all other needs. Order is the principle of their relations and limits in which each obligation encounters other obligations. More concretely, "the imperfection of a social order is measured by the quantity of situations" in which two obligations being incompatible, an individual is "forced to abandon one of them" (*L'Enracinement,* 11; NR, 4) in order to accomplish the other. Totalitarianism offers a pure example of this *disorder.* Totalitarian "order" is in reality a disorder, in which one cannot obey without violating freedom; nor can one establish a hierarchy without denying equality; one cannot bring about security without denying the need for risk or wish for freedom of expression without denying the fundamental need for truth . . . and reciprocally. Far from satisfying the nostalgia of a "party of order," *L'Enracinement* defines order as that which makes it possible for needs, hence obligations, to come to light in such a manner that no single one of them casts a shadow on any other.

Her reference then to the supernatural, which should impregnate this world, does not signify a flight from the social. Knowing that a plant lives by both light and water, and that it would be an "error to count on grace alone," *L'Enracinement* shows that "terrestrial energy is necessary as well" (*Oeuvres complètes* VI.4.418). The essay treats of the social and political energy indispensable to the *appearance* of institutions and public morality that permit the articulation of the spiritual and of material life. However, Weil underlines with equal force that it is necessary "to restrain to a minimum the part of the supernatural indispensable to making social life bearable. Whatever tends to increase this part is evil" (*Oeuvres complètes* VI.2.418). A spiritual dictatorship would mix together the social and the spiritual[13] levels in order to bring about a "sacral society," sought solely by integrists.

Despite the difficulty of the task, it must be determined on what real bases spirituality can become a vocation for all men, in the very conditions of their lives. Points of insertion must be found for absolute obligations with regard to the relative goods that these conditions represent. Uprooting (*déracinement*) is precisely the destruction of these social and cultural intermediary milieus,[14] which are points of passage toward transcendence and bridges leading down from transcendence, permitting the soul to rise and the supernatural to descend. The consequences of this uprooting consist in a shattering of meaning by the fragmentation of a culture that has turned pragmatic and foreign to reality. On the other hand, the setting of roots (*enracinement*) reestablishes multiple relationships with the world by means of the essential elements of our civilization. It is not a question of "re-enchanting" the world by a return to a pre-modern unification or to an artisanal mode of production. What must be avoided at all cost, in opposition to the privatization of meaning that transforms values into a matter of opinion or taste, is the re-establishment of a spiritual power giving structure to society. The world of the city is the very opposite of a "society with divine pretentions."[15]

Conclusion

Let us consider one more time the perfect imitator of God. How does he perceive the world? Simone Weil found an unequaled formulation for the answer: "He came out of his cave, he looked at the sun, and he went back into his cave. Timaeus is the book about a man going back into his cave. So the world of the senses no longer appears there as a cave" (*La Source grecque,* 129; SNL, 132). The world "becomes the opposite of a nightmare" (*Sur la science,* 249) for "the order of the world *is* beautiful" (*La Source grecque,* 129; SNL, 132). Or, as a passage in the notebooks says: "*Timeus.* The City inhabited by those who are in an awakened state. The world is no longer a subterranean prison" (*Oeuvres complètes* VI.2.445). "'In an awakened state' and not in a dream, as is the actual case," as Plato had already specified,[1] for the vision and action of the philosopher who has come back into the City confers on it a reality it did not have before.

However, this return also confers his own particular reality on him who goes back down into the cave: "The fullness of God's reality is outside this world, but the fullness of the reality of a man is in this world, even if that man were perfect"[2] (*Oeuvres complètes* VI.3.51). In a London notebook she states clearly: "Human obligations must be carried out within that framework of social relations in which one is found, unless there is a special commandment from God to go elsewhere" (*Oeuvres complètes* VI.4.363). The work of Simone Weil is a contemporary version of the "book about the man gone back into his cave" in the very conditions of our civilization, and her philosophy responds to the astonishment she expressed in her notebook: "A curious question about historic materialism: why is there such an absence of 'platonism' in our day?" (*Oeuvres complètes* VI.1.121). She sought to fill in this lacuna without ceding anything, either to platonism or to materialism. To escape from its disarray, an epoch like ours requires both a Marx "surpassed from the interior" by Plato, and a Plato who would have "integrated" Marx. Even when she called for a new form of sanctity, Weil sought a degree of combination corresponding to the ideal—"as unrealizable as a dream, but different from a dream in its relation to reality" (*Oeuvres complètes* II.2.72; OL, 84)—along with the demands made by the conditions of our existence in this world. "Today it is not enough just to be a saint, what is needed is a sanctity that the present moment demands, a new sanctity that is also without precedent" (*Attente de Dieu,* 81; WG, 51). She was, and she remained until the dawn of her spiritual period, a philosopher of the heartrending quest for mediations, a thinker in search of measure and equilibrium, who does not retreat in the face of what is violent in the contradictions that have the capacity to draw us upward. If there is a chance of drawing close to something real, in this world or beyond this world, that chance can be accorded only to those who run the risk of exposing themselves in thought as well as in action. Simone Weil always took this risk.

Her vocation took on a very original form in the history of philosophic thought. The "interior necessity" she spoke of in a letter to Simone Pétrement, a necessity from which she could not withdraw without betraying herself (*La Vie*, 578; SWL, 433), is never foreign to an enumeration of the historical and political events likely to make this interior necessity more and more powerful. This is why Weil could be nothing other than a philosopher exposed to the events of her time. With her the most visible torments and heartbreaks are evidence of the difficulty she experienced, less in following her particular vocation than in knowing what real mediations had to be adopted in the circumstances of the moment to carry out that vocation rather than to shatter it.[3] How was she to know which decision would permit the power of the laws of exterior necessity to sustain her interior necessity, all the while knowing very well that, detached from the conditions of their realization, all aspirations and any vocation would remain suspended in the unreal? Simone Weil gave a perfect illustration of this problem at the end of her *Carnet de Londres*, where she put down, in her staccato notebook style, a summary statement of her experience in this matter: "Philosophy . . . is something realized *exclusively* in action and practice—This is why it is so difficult to write about—Difficult like a treatise on tennis or foot races, only even more so" (*Oeuvres complètes* VI.4.392, emphasis by Simone Weil).

n o t e s

Notes to Chapter 1

1. She worked in the Alsthom factory, in the J-J. Carnaud Forges in Basse-Indre, and in the Renault factories.

2. Durruti directed the most important unit of the militia of the central union anarchists.

3. "Réflexions sur la barbarie" and "L'*Iliade* ou le poème de la force" (*Oeuvres*, 505–7; SE, 142–44 and *Oeuvres*, 527–52; SWR, 153–83).

4. See "A propos de la question coloniale dans ses rapports avec le destin du peuple français" (*Oeuvres*, 427–40).

5. Bergery, a radical politician, founded the Common Front against Fascism (1933). He voted in favor of full powers for Pétain.

6. See R. Chenavier, "Simone Weil, la 'haine juive de soi'?" *Cahiers Simone Weil* (December 1991): 291–328.

7. She wrote this also to Jean Wahl in October 1942 (*Oeuvres*, 977–78; SL, 157–61).

8. See Gilbert Kahn, "Simone Weil et le christianisme," in the collection he edited *Simone Weil. Philosophe, historienne et mystique* (Paris: Aubier Montaigne, 1978), 38.

9. "The good thief alone saw justice as Plato conceived it, discerned perfectly and nakedly under the appearance of a criminal" (*Intuitions préchrétiennes*, 84).

10. She gave this testimony in an interview with Wladimir Rabi, *Cahiers Simone Weil* (June 1981): 76–78.

11. "Experience de la vie d'usine," then "Conditions première d'un travail non servile" (*La Condition ouvrière,* 327–51 and 418–34).

12. See *Ecrits de Londres,* 185–87; *Oeuvres complètes* IV.1.401–11; and SL, 145–53 for the text of the project.

13. Maurice Schumann, "Présentation de Simone Weil," in *Simone Weil. Philosophe, historienne et mystique* (Paris: Aubier Montaigne, 1978), 22–23.

Notes to Chapter 2

1. The reign of Proteus is the reign of metamorphoses that hinder the formation of ideas of space and time. In mythology, Proteus delivers his predictions if he is bound in chains, but he ceaselessly changes form.

2. See "De la perception ou l'aventure de Protée," which appeared in *Libres Propos,* 5 (May 20, 1929) (*Oeuvres complètes* I, 121–39), and the whole first chapter of R. Chenavier, *Simone Weil. Une philosophie du travail* (Paris: Cerf, 2001).

3. "The scheme [is] the form of all our actions inasmuch as they have as their condition to be works, that is to say, not to be immediate" (*Oeuvres complètes* I, 154. See also Simone Weil's notes, pp. 147–58).

4. "To know anything at all in space, a line for example, I must draw it" (Kant, *Critique de la raison pure* [Paris: PUF, 1967], 115). This idea was taken up again by Lagneau and by Alain.

5. Gaston Bachelard, *La Terre et les Rêveries de la volonté* (Paris: Corti, 1973), 55.

6. "It is not outside some limit that one goes beyond his master, but within his very thought" (Alain, *Entretiens au bord de la mer,* in *Les Passions de la Sagesse* [Paris: Gallimard, 1960], 1359).

7. See the review, "Lenin, *Matérialisme et empirio-criticism*" (*Oeuvres complètes* II.1.306–7).

8. An expression borrowed from Kant (*Critique de la raison pure,* 205).

9. See the letter to Robert Guihéneuf (1936), *Cahiers Simone Weil* (March-June 1998): 1–20.

10. A method based on analogy would permit one to think without ceasing to perceive. See the letters to Guihéneuf, ibid., and to Alain, *Sur la science,* 114.

11. Alain, Letter to Simone Weil, June 28, 1935, *Bulletin de l'association des amis d'Alain* (June 1984): 28.

12. See Rolf Kühn, "Dimensions et logique interne de la pensée de Simone Weil," in *Simone Weil. Philosophe, historienne et mystique* (Paris: Aubier Montaigne, 1978), 338.

13. See *La Condition ouvrière,* 424, and *Oeuvres complètes* IV.1.307.

14. An article by Julius Dickmann (1895–1938?), "La véritable limite de la production capitaliste" (*La Critique sociale,* September 1933) influenced the composition of *Réflexions sur les causes de la liberté et de l'oppression sociale.*

15. Weil is taking aim here at the theoreticians of "L'ordre nouveau" (the New Order), Robert Aron and Arnaud Dandieu, authors of *La Révolution nécessaire* (Paris: Grasset, 1933). See her review in *Oeuvres complètes* II.1.324–28.

16. Cf. K. Marx, *Le Capital,* in *Oeuvres* II (Paris: Gallimard, 1968), 1487.

17. "When the victims of social oppression actually revolt, all my sympathies go to them, though not sustained by any hope; when a revolution ends in a partial success, I rejoice" (*La Condition ouvrière,* 232).

18. A letter to Souvarine gives an example (SL, 17).

19. In the course of this research Simone Weil came across the works of Jacques Lafitte. She read his *Réflexions sur la science des machines* that appeared in 1932 (republished by Vrin, 1972). She recalled especially his concept of "reflex machines" capable of reacting flexibly to the activity of an individual. See two letters sent to the engineer and a letter to Souvarine in *La Condition ouvrière,* 252–63.

Notes to Chapter 3

1. See "Is There a Marxist Doctrine?" (*Oppression et liberté,* 229; OL, 169).

2. See "Le materialism historique" (*Oeuvres complètes* II.1.330–31).

3. Kant, Letter to Mendelssohn, April 8, 1766 (*Oeuvres Philosophiques* [Paris: Gallimard, 1980], I, 603). The notion of progress according to Weil, like Kant's notion of happiness, borrows from experience elements that are not of the same nature.

4. *Oeuvres complètes* II.2.40, 77; OL, 50, 89–91.

5. The "inextricable mingling of the military and the economic" (*Oeuvres complètes* II.1.292) subordinates the economic sphere to the struggle for power. Weil was opposed to Marx's notion that the economy becomes a

determining factor when production, in its industrial form, is the indispensable means to develop the power of States. See *Oeuvres complètes* II.2.100–1; OL, 115–17.

6. To Hegel's dialectic, Weil opposed Plato's conception of a "movement of the soul" that "relies on the irreducible contradictions" that it encounters in order "to rise to a higher domain" (*Oppression et liberté*, 248–49; OL, 190; as well as *Oppression et liberté*, 208, 228; OL, 159–60, 173–74).

7. *Oeuvres complètes* VI.2.454. Weil continues: "There is no contradiction in the imaginary. Contradiction is the proof of necessity."

Notes to Chapter 4

1. She wrote to Joë Bousquet that "the very word God" had no place whatsoever in her thoughts "until the day when [she could] not refuse it to Him" (*Oeuvres,* 797).

2. Beauty is one of the processes of "decreation." See chapter 5 below.

3. See note 26 below.

4. This rejection is discussed in chapter 5 below.

5. See *Lettre à un religieux*, proposition 26.

6. "He" is the "visitor" of the "Prologue," a figure of Christ in this mystical prose poem, written apparently in 1941.

7. The general feeling of inadequacy (*Attente de Dieu,* 17; WG, 5–6) is the major element in Weil's interior agony, and not just on the religious level. Dominique-Marie Dauzet thinks that the "question 'how can He love me' is the exclamation of an entire life" ("Simone Weil, passion anorectique. vision eucharistique," *Les Enjeux philosophiques de la mystique,* collected by D. de Courcelles [Grenoble, Jérôme Millon. 2007], 135). See "Notes intimes" of Weil, *Oeuvres complètes* VI.1.144 and 407–8.

8. M. Broc-Lapeyre, "Que ma volonté soit défaite," and "Simone Weil et la mystique nihiliste," *Cahiers Simone Weil* (March 1986 and September 1999).

9. "Lettre à Gilbert Kahn," *Cahiers Simone Weil* (December 1995): 342.

10. One notebook establishes a list of twenty-seven "images of Christ" (*Oeuvres complètes* VI.4.224–25).

11. Simone Weil's idea of a Christianity "containing all vocations" might well be compared to the "inclusive" perspective of Jacques Dupuis, *Vers une théologie chrétienne du pluralisme religieux* and *La Rencontre du christianisme et des religions* (Paris: Cerf, 1997 and 2002).

12. Weil translates this expression as "while waiting" (*Attente de Dieu,* 54; WG, 32).

13. *Cahiers Simone Weil* (September 1981): 130–31. See "A letter to Jacques Maritain (July 1942)," *Cahiers Simone Weil* (June 1980): 68.

14. J. Daniélou, "Hellénisme, judaïsme, christianisme," in *Réponses aux questions de Simone Weil* (Paris: Aubier Montaigne, 1964), 35.

15. On this subject, see *Oeuvres complètes* IV.1.352 and 371, as well as *Intuitions pré-chrétiennes*, 78 and 84.

16. "Being a creature does not necessarily mean suffering affliction, but it does necessarily mean being exposed to affliction" (*Oeuvres complètes* IV.1.369).

17. However, when affliction fell upon the Jews, Weil did not see the Cross in this as Edith Stein and Jacques Maritain did.

18. J.-M. Perrin, Introduction to *Attente de Dieu* (Paris: Du Vieux Colombier, 1950), 32.

19. The first ten propositions and propositions 29 to 35 of the *Lettre à un religieux* confirm her refusal of the Old Testament revelation.

20. Islam would be an example of the same refusal of the Mediator. In the Koran, Allah is also the "God of the Bedouin army." On the other hand, "The Beloved of the mystics of the 10th century is not that Allah. He is the Mediator" (*Oeuvres complètes* VI.3.297).

21. Essays published respectively in *Oeuvres complètes* IV.1.375–89, and in *Pensées sans ordre*, 47–62.

22. Her letter to J. Wahl enumerates the historical trends in which Weil detected the expression of an "identical thought . . . expressed with scarcely varying modalities" (*Oeuvres,* 979*).*

23. This is the case with Paul Giniewski, *Simone Weil ou la haine de soi* (Paris: Berg International, 1978) and George Steiner, *De la Bible à Kafka* (Paris: Bayard, 2002). For a recent clarification, see the dossier "Simone Weil antisémite? Un sujet qui fache?" *Cahiers Simone Weil* (September 2007).

24. An expression used by Weil in her "spiritual autobiography" (*Attente de Dieu*, 47; WG, 28).

25. See J.-M. Perrin, *Mon Dialogue avec Simone Weil* (Paris: Nouvelle Cité, 1984), 115.

26. According to D.-M. Dauzet (see note 7 above), the formula "the thought of the Passion of Christ entered into me" is to be understood literally. Simone Weil wanted to "live the passion itself, to make herself a host instead of receiving the host in the Eucharist." The metaphor of the hunger of the soul gradually invades her work, but, while in this world, "it is not

possible to look and to eat at the same time . . . in the supernatural world, the soul 'through contemplation eats the truth'" (*Oeuvres complètes* VI.3.159). Weil must have felt the need to "remain hungry." On the one hand, hunger is a "relationship to food certainly less complete than the act of eating, but just as real." On the other hand, however, she felt certain that for a being like her, with her particular vocation, "it is perhaps not inconceivable that . . . the desire for and the privation of the sacraments might constitute a purer contact than participation itself" (*Attente de Dieu*, 27; WG, 13).

27. This is based on the testimony given by Canon Vidal (letters of 1955 to Simone Pétrement, "Simone Weil Archives," Bibliothèque nationale de France. See *La Vie*, 606–7; SWL, 456–57).

28. What position would Weil have adopted after the Second Vatican Council? Father Perrin thought that a great number of her objections would have vanished (*Comme un veilleur attend l'aurore* [Paris: Cerf, 1998], 143–44). A different point of view is presented, with solid support, by André Naud (*Les Dogmes et le Respect de l'intelligence. Plaidoyer inspiré par Simone Weil* [Saint-Laurent, Quebec: Fides, 2002], final chapter).

Notes to Chapter 5

1. See *Oeuvres complètes* IV.1.337; SWR, 492.

2. One of the consequences of this thesis is the refusal to introduce into personal life or into history a Providence conceived as a personal intervention by God into the sequence of causes of which each one is the effect of another in an indefinite series. (See *L'Enracinement,* 329ff and 351ff; NR, 262ff and 279ff.)

3. We take our inspiration here from Miklos Vetö, *La Métaphysique religieuse de Simone Weil* (Paris: Vrin, 1971; re-issued by L'Harmattan, 1997), chapter 1.

4. Weil's brackets.

5. Reminder of a verse by Homer, used as an epigraph for the *Journal d'usine:* "Very much in spite of yourself, under pressure of a cruel necessity" (FW, 155*).* See *La Condition ouvrière*, 81.

6. André-A. Devaux, "Le Christ dans la vie et dans l'oeuvre de Simone Weil," *Cahiers Simone Weil* (June 1981): 104. Daniel Cadrin thinks that, refusing to believe in an afterlife, Weil remained "on the threshold, on that Holy Saturday of waiting" ("Simone Weil et la critique des idoles," *La Vie spirituelle* [Cerf, September 1999], 463).

7. This is what we are led to believe by certain passages in her letter to Joë Bousquet, totally immobilized until his death in 1950 by a wound he received during the First World War (*Oeuvres,* 794).

8. See "Réflexions sur le bon usage des etudes scolaires en vue de l'amour de Dieu" (*Oeuvres complètes* IV.1.255–62; SWS, 91–106).

9. See *L'Enracinement,* 371; NR, 295.

10. Weil encountered obstacles when she tried to lay the foundations of a spirituality of work under the conditions of industrial production. She sketched out her reflections on intermediary elements that can direct the soul toward the supernatural, rhythm, for example, which—like dancing, with movements that are directed without being constrained from the exterior—is capable of leading to decreative attention. See R. Chenavier, *Simone Weil. Une philosophie du travail,* 483ff and 592ff.

11. Weil makes an embarrassing use of the word 'supernatural'. She uses it in the ordinary sense: that which surpasses the level of nature and rises to the level of divine action. Within us, it is a "living being other than ourselves, a divine being" (*Oeuvres complètes* VI.3.336). She also wishes to treat the supernatural as a "scientific notion" (*L'Enracinement,* 370; NR, 294). Thus we find that John of the Cross described "the operation of grace on the soul with the precision of a chemist or a geologist" (*Oppression et liberté,* 219; OL, 167). The supernatural operates by procedures that are "more precise, more vigorous than the crude mechanism of matter" (*Oeuvres complètes* VI.4.83). There is a "logic of supernatural reason . . . more rigorous than that of natural reason" (*Oeuvres complètes* VI.4.139). This supernatural reason, however, does not exist except in "souls that burn with supernatural love of God."

12. See her writings in the section on "Science" in the *Oeuvres complètes* IV.1.139–210; SNL, 3–43. The stake in the criticism of contemporary science by Weil is to find out under what conditions a science can furnish an "image of the world," such as is found in other domains (religion, mythology, art). But contemporary physics loses any possible representation of the world by its combination of algebraic signs about which one wonders to what reality they refer and what meaning they have.

13. Patrice Rolland, who is a jurist, is right to ask if when she passes from the institutional application of her theory on the articulation of the supernatural and the social, Weil does not misconstrue the specificities of politics and of law. Doesn't she surrender to a "moralistic reduction of the law" and to a "penalization of political life," which could end up in a government of judges? See "Simone Weil and the Law," *Cahiers Simone Weil* (September 1990): 244ff.

14. On uprooting (*déracinement*) and its conseqences, see *L'Enracinement*, 63–233 (NR, 43–184) and P. Rolland, "Approche politique de *L'Enracinement*," *Cahiers Simone Weil* (December 1983): 304ff.

15. "A society with pretentions to being divine, like the Church, is perhaps even more dangerous by the ersatz good that it contains than by the evil that besmirches it. . . . A divine label on something that is social: an inebriating mixture that contains every form of license. The Devil in disguise" (*Oeuvres complètes* VI.2.419. See pp. 418–21 on the distinction between the social and the City).

Notes to the Conclusion

1. Plato, *The Republic*, VII.520c.

2. Without even taking into account the central place she accorded to the beauty of the world, this citation alone would suffice to refute any interpretation of the thought of Weil as a form of gnosticism.

3. Let us think for example of the painful hesitations expressed in a letter to Father Perrin, when she was about to leave Marseille (*Attente de Dieu*, 30–33; WG, 17–19). See R. Chenavier, Foreword to the *Oeuvres complètes* IV.1.41–42.

s e l e c t e d b i b l i o g r a p h y

Pétrement, Simone. *La vie de Simone Weil.* Paris: Fayard, 1973.

————. *Simone Weil, A Life.* Translated by Raymond Rosenthal. NewYork: Pantheon Books, 1976.

Weil, Simone. *Attente de Dieu.* Introduction by J.-Marie Perrin. Paris: Vieux Colombier, 1950. Re-edition, Fayard, 2006 (without the introduction of the first edition).

————. *La Condition ouvrière.* Introduction and notes by R. Chenavier. Paris: Gallimard, 2002.

————. *Ecrits de Londres et dernières lettres.* Paris: Gallimard, 1957.

————. *Ecrits historiques et politiques.* Paris: Gallimard, 1960.

————. *L'Enracinement.* Paris: Gallimard, 1949.

————. *Formative Writings, 1929–1941.* Edited and translated by Dorothy Tuck McFarland and Wilhelmina Van Ness. Amherst: University of Massachusetts Press, 1987.

————. *Intimations of Christianity among the Ancient Greeks.* Boston: Beacon Press, 1957.

————. *Intuitions pre-chrétiennes.* Paris: Fayard, 1985.

————. *La Source Grecque.* Paris: Gallimard, 1953.

————. *Letter to a Priest.* London: Routledge & Kegan Paul, 1953.

————. *Lettre à un Religieux.* Paris: Seuil, 1974.

————. *The Need for Roots.* Translated by Arthur Wills. Boston: Beacon Press, 1952.

————. *Oeuvres.* Short works (1929–1943) collected by F. de Lussy. Paris: Gallimard, 1999.

res complètes. Edited by André-A Devaux and Florence de Lussy. vols. Paris: Gallimard, 1988–

Science, Necessity, and the Love of God. Essays collected, trans- and edited by Richard Rees. London: Oxford University Press,

Oppression and Liberty. Translated by Arthur Wills and John Petrie. erst: University of Massachusetts Press, 1973.

———. *Oppression et liberté.* Paris: Gallimard, 1955.

———. *Pensées sans ordre concernant l'amour de Dieu.* Paris: Gallimard, 1962.

———. *Selected Essays, 1934–1943.* Translated by Richard Rees. London: Oxford University Press, 1962.

———. *Seventy Letters.* Translated by Richard Rees. London: Oxford University Press, 1965.

———. *Simone Weil.* Writings selected and introduced by Eric O. Springsted. Maryknoll, NY: Orbis Books, 1998.

———. *Simone Weil, An Anthology.* Edited and introduced by Siân Miles. New York: Weidenfeld & Nicolson, 1986.

———. *The Simone Weil Reader.* New York: David McKay, 1981.

———. *Sur la Science.* Paris: Gallimard, 1966.

———. *Waiting for God.* Translated by Emma Craufurd. New York: Harper & Row, 2001.